AF352623

George S. Counts
and
Charles A. Beard

SUNY Series in the Philosophy of Education

Philip L. Smith, Editor

George S. Counts
and
Charles A. Beard

Collaborators for Change

Lawrence J. Dennis

State University of New York Press

Published by
State University of New York Press, Albany

For information, address State University of New York
Press, State University Plaza, Albany, N.Y., 12246

Library of Congress Cataloging-in-Publication Data

Dennis, Lawrence J.
    George S. Counts and Charles A. Beard, collaborators for change /
Lawrence J. Dennis.
        p.   cm. — (SUNY series in the philosophy of education)
    Half title: George S. Counts and Charles A. Beard.
    Bibliography: p.
    Includes index.
    ISBN 0-88706-992-4.   ISBN 0-88706-993-2 (pbk.)
    1. Counts, George S. (George Sylvester), 1889-1974.   2. Beard,
Charles Austin, 1874-1948.   3. Educators—United States—Biography.
4. Historians—United States—Biography.   I. Title.   II. Series.
LB885.C662D45 1989
370'.92'2—dc19   88-20153
                                                                      CIP

10 9 8 7 6 5 4 3 2 1

For W.E.E. in Friendship

Contents

Acknowledgments

It is as difficult to let a manuscript leave one's hands as it is to send one's children to college. But all must make off, leaving us somewhat lonely and vulnerable. Thus, after many years of living with George Counts and Charles Beard, I have sent these pages to their excellent publisher. One's children, for better or worse, are largely what one has made them; and so is this book, with its limitations, as well as, I trust, its strengths.

One does not raise one's children entirely alone. They have characters even at birth. Counts and Beard were there for me to find, and I am immeasurably richer for their company. Children also have friends and mentors. I have too — those who have helped me with this book in ways both great and small, and whom I thank with sincerity. First among these are the heirs of my two protagonists, who have generously given me permission to quote extensively from private correspondence: Dr. Martha Counts, Dr. Detlev Vagts, and Miss Arlene Beard.

Over the years, I have gathered materials from several libraries: Morris Library, Southern Illinois University at Carbondale; Walter Library, University of Minnesota; Joseph Regenstein Library, the University of Chicago; Roy O. West Library, DePauw University; and the Library of Congress. Their staffs were uniformly cooperative; I would like particularly to acknowledge the contributions of Maxine Clapp, Alan Cohn, Ruth Bauner, Lorene Pixley, and David Koch and his associates. From these men and women I have learned much concerning the care with which our country's written heritage is preserved. Others who have held my hand and helped me over fences include Donald L. Beggs, Harry G. Miller, Jo Ann Boydston, Eugene F. Provenzo, Jr., Philip L Smith, Rosemary Timke, Justin Dennis, and William Edward Eaton, to whom this book is dedicated. Becky Molina-Shappard is not only a wonderful typist, but also has the uncanny ability of turning hieroglyphics into words.

To my wife, Maureen, and our four sons, who dropped tools, loaded the car (heavily), and moved to Toronto for a semester, where this work was first pulled into shape (and subsequently pulled out again and again), my love and gratitude.

Lawrence J. Dennis
Carbondale, Illinois
September 1988

Introduction

Charles A. Beard and George S. Counts were important figures in the intellectual milieu of America in its passage through the twentieth century. The justification for this book lies in the prominence of the central characters, who wrestled with some of the weighty matters of education and their relationship to what they, and others, believed to be an emerging social order. This is the story of the relationship between Beard and Counts as they collaborated to bring about substantial changes in American education. They did not hatch a plot, although, as will be seen, some thought they did. Rather, they were working out the intellectual base of what came to be known as social reconstructionism. C.A. Bowers states that Beard was "loosely associated with the social reconstruction group."[1] It will be shown here that the association was actually much tighter. Gerald Gutek suggests as much when he writes, "The historical perspective from which Counts developed his social and educational policies was essentially Beardian."[2] This is the premise of the book. It traces the collaboration of Counts and Beard as Counts tried to impress upon teachers of the nation the importance of interpreting the present in the context of the past, and of then making plans for shaping the future in view of what he saw to be the unfulfilled promises of America.

But educational change is not easy to bring about in a free society. The compulsions of communism that were put to use in Russia when Counts made his visits there are not available to us. The polemics of politicians, even if they can supply financial inducements, are weak. The persuasions of educational and other intel-

1

lectual leaders are even weaker, although they may have some slight and generalized influences over time. Larry Cuban, who has written recently about teachers and teaching, has looked at constancy and change in American education. Adapting the distinctions made by Paul Watzlawick and associates, he talks about first-order and second-order changes. The former are small, nonstructural, and unimportant; the latter are large, lasting, and fundamental. Counts and Beard wanted second-order changes. They, along with many of their peers, called on the schools and teachers to recognize the realities of the twentieth century, as they saw them, and to reorganize schooling on the lines that will be discussed later. They stressed the importance of planning, social cooperation, the common good, and a global perspective. Later, Counts called for recognition of the educational implications of the atomic age, and Beard was among the first to realize their import. To accommodate such concerns necessitated second-order changes, although neither men described in detail what those changes should be. Counts did call for teacher militancy and a unified sense of purpose, and Beard urged teachers to take stands. Both looked to the unions to provide leadership.

It is possible that Counts and Beard did accomplish second-order changes. They changed our thinking. Beard's historiography may not be acceptable today, but his influence was so far-reaching that history will never be viewed in quite the same way again. That is true, too, of the work of George Counts. Social reconstructionism is no longer fashionable (although one could make the case, as Counts himself did, that all education is a form of social reconstruction one way or another), but the work of Counts has changed the way we look at education.

Beard was, of course, primarily a historian, not an educator in the formal sense, and he used history as a tool for understanding the present. The events of history were, for him, not inert data, but were able to teach us values to which we could appropriately subscribe. If the lessons of history can enable us to discern and direct contemporary values, it follows then that the role of education must be absolutely fundamental. Here, Beard's ideas were similar to those of his younger contemporary. As Gutek writes, "Counts used the new history, especially Beard's version, to create a frame of reference for his theory of cultural reconstruction. His use of the new history was ideological in that it furnished a historical rationale for his projected new social order. The frame of reference that the new history provided was a selective perspective of America's past that was to be put to work as an ideological instrument to create a particular vision of America's future."[3] This was precisely what Beard himself tried to do. Richard Hofstadter mentions the "capacity that Beard would always have in generous measure for a selective use of historical facts in order to put across his message."[4] Again, Hofstadter, referring to Beard, writes, "[H]e was too much the social activist to shake off his feeling that historical knowledge, however 'scientifically' it was gained, ought to serve the common weal by being made to shed light on the origins and the solution of contemporary problems, and that for this purpose it would have to be translated into moral terms."[5] He could have been writing about George Counts.

Counts's experiences in Russia in the late 1920s and his return to New York immediately following the cataclysmic effects of the beginning of the depression might well have caused him to espouse a Marxist point of view, had he not found a better way. Economics may drive history, but not necessarily along the deterministic lines of Marx. Beard himself had already offered an alternative in his *Economic Interpretation of the Constitution*. Of this important work, Hofstadter writes, "The influence of Beard's book seems in retrospect singularly long-lived for a work so controversial and, as it has proved, so vulnerable. . . . The Great Depression and the renewed social struggle of the New Deal era only created a still more receptive climate of opinion for it."[6] Counts was among the most receptive.

Whether or not Counts was saved from falling for Marxism by his association with Beard, he was labelled a "red" by Hearst and others during the 1930s. Yet his FBI files reveal that, although he was investigated, largely as a result of some smear letters written to Director Hoover, the bureau was not too worried about Counts's loyalties. In fact, as the decade closed, it was Counts who was directly responsible for clearing the New York locals of the American Federation of Teachers (AFT) of communist influences. Shortly after, further public proclamation was made of his anticommunism when he left the American Labor Party (ALP) which he chaired, to become an active agent in founding the Liberal Party of New York State, which was formed largely in protest against the communist insurgence into the ALP. There is little doubt that any flirtation with Marxism on Counts's part would have disappeared by the late 1930s anyway, but in Beard's use of history he found the basis for his own form of social reconstructionism. Thus the usefulness of a Marxist interpretation of history was obviated. The shape of the future was not, as Marx believed, predetermined; that depended for Counts and Beard upon the goals to be striven for and the values aspired to. Counts held, as did Dewey, that the accumulated past is all we have to deal with the present, and thus the views of Beard and Counts with respect to the goods of society and the role of education in achieving them coincided.

Beard, for his part, modified his views throughout the thirties; this was the period of his close association with Counts. Again Hofstadter: "His vision of progress . . . had always been rooted in his rationalism, his faith in the ultimate sway of material forces. . . . Now, more and more, as the Great Depression and the fear of a new war loomed larger in his thoughts, he relapsed from his role of Olympian observer of an inevitable progress and gave way to the prophet in himself, to his hortatory role, to his interest in the manipulative function of historical ideas. . . . But now it became clear to him that historical writing . . . must serve activist criticism and forge a social idealism consonant with the needs of the hour"[7] Hofstadter also writes, "The unifying and sustaining thread in his conception of history was that it ought to be an agency of social improvement."[8] That is exactly how Counts himself perceived the school—as an agency for social improvement. He wrote, "[T]he school should be regarded . . . as an agency for the abolition of all artificial social distinctions and of organizing the energies of the nation for the promotion of the general welfare."[9] It will become clear that Beard influenced Counts, but it also is probable that Counts influenced Beard.

Counts himself became less objective as the years went by. His former teacher, Charles Hubbard Judd, castigated him for this tendency: "I shall go down to my grave an enemy of the course in philosophy which you and others seem to want. My only advice to you is don't become a philosopher so long as you are young enough to make valuable contributions to factual knowledge. . . . Philosophy is too easy; beware of the enticements of this kind of thinking."[10] However, the imperatives of the present situation, as Counts saw it, demanded that he use the facts selectively. Beard, too, was caught in a similar dilemma. Again Hofstadter: "[H]e had a divided mind about the role of the historian. On the one hand, he believed that history ought to be an instrument of social criticism and social progress; on the other, that the historian or political scientist should be governed by the idea of scientific detachment and stay clear of moral judgments."[11] Thus, in a very real way, both Beard and Counts were wrestling with similar problems. Their training as social scientists collided with their natural feelings of compassion and concern.

By the end of the 1930s, economic issues were overtaken by the looming prospect of war. Counts and Beard reacted differently. Counts, fifteen years younger and institutionally based, threw himself into the war effort and preparations for the hoped-for peace; Beard retreated into isolationism. But during the critical period of their close association, it is clear that there was a mutual reinforcement.

Beard and Counts did not live in ivory towers. Both translated their beliefs into personal action, and, in Counts's case, into overt political action. Both came to see many of the problems that those of us who live through the last decades of the twentieth century and beyond will have to confront. Neither was completely convinced that they would be confronted successfully. Counts, in restating H.G. Wells's phrase that human history is a race between education and catastrophe, did not conclude that education would win; Beard was even less optimistic. In one of his last letters to Counts, written partly in response to the receipt of an article by Counts, Beard writes "The sky is clear and ominous: only two mighty armed powers are on the horizon. What impends and with what portents? Day and night, I wonder and tremble for the future of my country and mankind."[12] He wrote these words before the first atomic bombs were dropped.

Beard's growing disenchantment with Roosevelt, particularly as it centered around the entry of America into the Second World War, brought forth much hostility, and lost him the respect and even friendship of many of his former colleagues. He was convinced that America's entry into the war would be followed by imperialist expansion, the growth of the military, and the inevitable debasement of all he cherished in democratic values. The fears he expressed concerning the powers of the executive and the spread of official secrecy, both of which he believed to be at odds with the true principles of democracy, can now be seen as wondrously perceptive regardless of whether or not one believes America had the responsibility to free the world of fascism. But the focus of this record is not attached primarily to Beard as a historian—but to Beard as an educator. To this little attention has been paid. In Ellen Nore's intellectual biography of Beard,[13] and in Bernard C. Borning's *Political and Social Thought of Charles A. Beard,*[14] this facet of his work has been virtually omitted. In fact, both make no mention of the Commission on the Social Studies, and only refer briefly to Counts. Therefore, this book will help to"round out" the portrait of this man of principle. At the same time, it should bring into sharper relief the work of Counts, as we see him wrestling with a point of view, turning to his older friend for counsel (and sometimes getting more than he bargained for), and trying to reshape our conception of education in this new age.

Counts-Beard Correspondence

When George S. Counts died on November 10, 1974, just a few weeks short of his eighty-fifth birthday, he left a few boxes of miscellaneous papers. Three years earlier, upon his retirement from Southern Illinois University at Carbondale, he gave a small collection of papers to the Special Collections of the Morris Library. Counts confessed that he destroyed the bulk of his papers when he left Teachers College in 1955 after a career there of almost thirty years. It is said that he did this in an uncharacteristic state of pique at being "put out to pasture" with so many productive years ahead of him. The story fits, for most of what he left at the end in those boxes were more recent papers, as for instance a collection of congratulatory messages on his eightieth birthday. But there were other things. It might be safe to assume that these "other things" included some too precious to have been destroyed earlier. This assumption works. His Russian diary is there, as is a short , privately printed booklet on the ancestry of the Counts (originally Kuntz) family, of Black Dutch (Germanic) origin. There is a photograph of the young Counts as Dionysus—strong-jawed and determined-looking—in *The Frogs,* and the opening chapters of his early book, never completed, which was to have been called *The Story of Human Progress.* Among those few items given to the Morris Library by Counts himself that predated his Teachers College retirement is his correspondence with Charles A. Beard. Martha Counts recalls that she talked her father out of destroying the letters, which stand as a record not only of a collaboration and a friendship but also of a back-stage view of some events of the 1930s that were significant at the time, and remain so.

For his part, Beard and his wife, Mary, kept very few personal, or for that matter impersonal, documents. The Beard papers at DePauw University contain a mere handful of letters. Beard is reported to have stated that he wanted to be judged by his work and not by what he had eaten for breakfast. Nevertheless, we do know Beard in many ways, for he was a man whose controversial writings and principled actions drew the spotlight of publicity. As a result, he is easier to know than George Counts.

In his old age, Counts recalled his friendship with Beard: "I think Charlie Beard thought I was an agreeable person, and I thought he was too." He chuckled, and, quoting Disraeli, said, "My opinion of an agreeable person is a person who agrees with me."[15] And, on the whole, it does seem that they were fundamentally in agreement over many matters. Some people have suggested that Beard was manipulating Counts,[16] but that view seems unwarranted on the basis of these letters. Counts himself states, "[f]rom the very first we found that we shared many common concerns and interests"[17] The correspondence certainly reveals an accord on basic issues, with Beard acting very much as the wise father to Counts's more headstrong youth. It is almost complete, with a few obvious gaps, most notably letters from the middle 1940s from Counts. Apart from these exceptions, Counts kept copies of most of his own letters to Beard, typed sometimes but not always by his competent secretary, Nucia Perlmutter Lodge, whereas Beard's letters were usually either typed by himself or written in longhand. Counts's were carefully dated, as by any good secretary, whereas Beard's were frequently dated by day and month only, without the year. Most are easy to date accurately; there remain few that cannot be dated.

The letters contain little personal matter—a few best wishes to Mrs. Beard, an occasional reference to Mrs. Counts, nothing at all about the children except as they pertain to William Beard's professional expertise; on both sides there is a personal warmth that shines through. The emotional climax of the letters comes when Beard begins, "Dear George—my beloved Son."[18] That was no mere figure of speech, and, in a lengthy interview conducted long after Beard's death, Counts recalled his friendship with Beard, and repeated with pride that "he regarded me as his son." But this outburst of warmth is only in its degree uncommon; one detects its growth in the tone of the letters as they move initially from formal inquiry and response to sincere regard.

The letters become less frequent as the occasions for close cooperation are removed. Beard, increasingly deaf and now suffering from eye trouble, but still very active, moves into the last years of his enormously productive and influential life, and Counts gets caught up in the political fray, with its attendant demands both of energy and time. Mary Beard writes the last letters in the collection.

As just mentioned, the letters deal barely at all with matters personal; rather, they deal with substantive issues that are most interesting to those familiar with and involved in education, particularly, of course, in education of the 1930s. The correspondence begins in 1929 and runs through 1946, but the bulk of the letters are from 1930 to 1938. They taper off as Counts becomes involved in the American Federation of Teachers and other overtly political activities. Their genesis is the membership of both men on the Commission on the Social Studies of the American Historical Association, and many of the letters revolve around their concerns as members of that commission. Indeed, we have a behind-the-scenes look at some of the activities and interests of the so-called left-wing group of the educational progressives. It will be up to the reader to decide whether these people saw events clearly.

Counts

George Sylvester Counts was born near Baldwin, Kansas, on December 9, 1889, and set his heart early on becoming a trapper. Instead, he entered Baker University, majoring in classics. His friend and colleague, John L. Childs, who must have got his information directly from Counts, writes, "Although courses in education were offered at Baker, Counts had not enrolled in any of them since at that time he had no thought of becoming a teacher."[19] In fact, he became engaged to Lois Bailey, and found himself teaching science and math at high school, and coaching athletics. A year later he became a teaching principal.

Counts had lost the chance of a Rhodes scholarship, since the previous year's winner had also come from Baker. He was, however, awarded a scholarship in sociology at the University of Chicago. Although he moved into education shortly after his arrival at Chicago, his main interests remained in the social studies. His teachers were among the most distinguished in their fields: Albion Small, Frederick Starr, and Charles E. Merriam. His major advisor was the noted psychologist Charles Hubbard Judd, and Counts was the first student to receive a doctorate from Chicago with a major in education and a minor in sociology.[20]

After graduation Counts moved around rapidly—Delaware College, Harris Teachers College in St. Louis, the University of Washington, and Yale. In 1926 he returned to the University of Chicago at Judd's request in order to launch a program in educational sociology, but he remained there for only one year. In 1927 he went to Teachers College, where he quickly became one of the leading and most controversial members of the faculty.

George Counts retired from Teachers College in 1955 at the age of sixty-five. With few exceptions that was the regulation at Columbia University; thus forced retirement did not come as a surprise. Either Counts was psychologically ill-prepared for it, or he thought that perhaps he, like Dewey, might have been accorded special dispensation to remain on the faculty. He was still productive and still a major force in educational and political circles. Although President Hollis Caswell permitted Counts to retain his office and secretary in order to finish work on his award-winning book, *The Challenge of Soviet Education*,[21] Counts left Teachers College, where he had been a distinguished member of the faculty for twenty-seven years. It was not to be a retirement—that did not come until 1971—and his plan to raise azaleas on his fifty-acre farm in Bucks County, Pennsylvania, was not realized. He was back in the educational fray almost immediately, and held visiting appointments at four institutions before going to Southern Illinois University in 1963.

Beard

Charles Austin Beard was born in 1874, and was just fifteen years older than Counts. He was raised on an Indiana farm, and, like Counts, was a child of preindustrial, rural, midwestern America. His was a long-standing Republican family. After graduation from DePauw in 1898, Beard spent almost four years in Europe, most of the time in England. He helped found Ruskin Hall at Oxford for students from the "working class" and was a familiar of many of the new socialists, including the future prime minister, Ramsey MacDonald. He returned briefly to America in 1900 for one term's study at Cornell. During this visit he married Mary Ritter who had been a fellow student at DePauw. Mary and Charles's relationship seems to have been cemented when Mary fell out of a boat rowed by Charles as it went over Eel River Falls a few miles south of Greencastle. The young couple removed to Europe, and, after a tour of the continent, settled in Oxford until 1902, when they returned to the States. Charles Beard received his Ph.D. from Columbia in 1904 and taught there until his resignation in 1917. With John Dewey, Thorstein Veblen, and James Harvey Robinson, he founded the New School of Social Research in 1919; two years later he founded the Workers' Education Bureau. He then became director of the Training School for Public Service. In its way, Beard's was a life of public service. Eric Goldman, writing of Beard's generation and specifically of Beard, says, "[I]t was the good fortune of Beard, and of so many of his generation, that they could speak of love of their country without embarrassment, and it was their glory that they identified American nationalism with incessant pursuit of a better-fed, better-housed, better-educated, and—above all—a genuinely and richly emancipated American people."[22]

Politics, Religion, and Home

Beard and Counts were ideological mavericks. Both were intensely patriotic (although charges to the contrary were made against them). Both saw things from a world perspective—Beard's stemming in part from his youthful study at Oxford, and Counts's from his interest in Soviet Russia. It seems apparent that both men flirted with Marxism. Beard had been introduced to the works of Marx by his teacher of history at DePauw, Colonel James Riley Weaver. In connection with one of Weaver's courses he spent the summer of 1896 in Chicago and lodged close to Jane Addam's Hull House. He was shocked by the effects of raw industrialism as he saw for the first time the misery of slum life. This experience gave him sympathy for the lot of the working class, which took practical form during his years at Oxford with his involvement in the work of Ruskin Hall. Beard had been introduced to the writings of John Ruskin by a high school teacher, Wilson Terrell. For a while Beard carried around with him a copy of Ruskin's polemical essays on unemployment and wages, *Unto This Last*. An etching of Ruskin hung over his typing desk in his New Milford home. Certainly in his early years Beard presented himself sometimes as a socialist, and one could build a strong case that Counts never did abandon altogether his adherence to socialism. One writer described Beard as "a pragmatic reformer" more than a socialist, and that is how one could properly describe Counts, who called himself a "cross between a Jeffersonian Democrat and a Lincoln Republican."[23] Both men were profoundly affected by the changes wrought by technology. In his later years Beard was reported to manifest "a noteworthy display of affection for the simple virtues of agrarian America."[24] He himself wrote, "Life was hard, but as I recall it all through the mists of time it seems beautiful against the wars, hatred, and intolerance of this age; and the best of the old days I should like to recover, for America and for the world."[25] Counts's oft-recounted tales of his young days, when trapping was for him not just a pastime but an eagerly anticipated occupation, were told with obvious relish. The pivot of his educational thought was his conviction, amply demonstrable, that his life spanned the greatest watershed in America's history—the move from an agrarian to an industrial society.

In noting some commonalities between Beard and Counts, some reference to the religions of their early years must be made. Beard's father was known as a freethinker, but he required that Charles, and his older brother Clarence, attend the Friends' services with him. Some say that Beard toyed with the idea of becoming a preacher in his DePauw days. The records of his fraternity there, Phi Gamma Delta, reveal Beard leading the membership "in prayer" on many occasions. He also expounded to the group on his theory of God. However, his "interesting paper," "Theosophy the New Religion," was probably more to his taste. In fact, a classmate of Beard emphasized that religion was not a factor in Beard's life while at DePauw. Counts was brought up a Methodist but seems to have disavowed any church connection by the time he reached young manhood. His wife, Lois, was the daughter of a Methodist minister. When asked just a few weeks before his death what his thoughts were on religion he denied that he had any. It appeared to be a topic totally without interest to him. However, he loved to sing the old Methodist hymns he had learned as a boy, and the organswell of the language of the King James Bible was apparent in his writing. Beard's association with Quakers also taught him about "the majestic dreams of the Jews, the merciful teaching of Jesus, and the sonorous roll of the King James version."[26] Both had an impressive command of the English language, which they spoke not only with vigor but with a noble beauty.

Beard and Counts sought retreat from city life in their country homes. Beard's more or less permanent home was in New Milford, Connecticut, and he spent the summer months usually in North Carolina; for Counts his Bucks County, Pennsylvania, house was an escape from the bustle of New York City. Counts found pleasure adorning his property with plants and trees brought from all over the world; Beard actually ran two dairy farms which shipped three hundred thousand quarts of milk a year, and he took the occupation very seriously. Reports vary as to how successful the farms were, but when asked whether he was making a profit, he replied, "Well, as a matter of fact I don't lose everything."[27] During the early depression years, the governor of Connecticut, Wilber L. Cross, who by virtue of having been dean of the Graduate School at Yale was an academic acquaintance of Beard, asked him to act as a mediator when the dairymen threatened a strike. The strike, set for August 17, 1933, was called off five days earlier, and on the 29th of that month Beard drafted a five-page report for the governor. Beard subsequently published an article on the situation facing the Connecticut dairy farmers. All this was a far cry from Counts's azaleas, but he may well have been influenced by Beard in his idealization of the life of the gentleman farmer.

Views on History

The similarities in background and interest between Beard and Counts should not be pushed too far—they serve no purpose save to demonstrate that the relationship between Charles Beard and George Counts was based not simply on mutual regard but also on certain similarities in points of view. However, one major similarity needs to be brought out clearly, for it was this, perhaps more than a certain commonality in background and belief, and a personal affinity, that accounts for the closeness between Counts and Beard. Beard believed any objective study of history to be impossible. The past is constantly interpreted in the light of the present and possible future. It was his book, *An Economic Interpretation of the Constitution of the United States,*[28] that caused controversy within the fraternity of historians. Beard's absence from the meetings of the American Historical Association from 1916 until 1933 perhaps reflects his isolation. Counts later discussed the book during the 1960s:

> Well, this book was published in 1913 and it aroused tremendous controversy.... And we see stressed economic forces or factors involved. Of course he told me one time, he had told others that there were 14 possible interpretation[s] in the U.S. He didn't say that this was the interpretation of the constitution, but an economic interpretation. There could have been many other interpretations, but he stressed economic. Again shortly before he died in the early 1940's in discussing this book with him and I put this question to him. If you were writing your economic interpretation today would it be different. Yes, it would be very different. I wrote that if the constitution's convention had been held in the 20th century, when it was held as a

matter of fact at the end of the 18th century, but since I was writing it as if it had occurred in the 20th century, I made it appear to be a very conservative document. Well, as a matter of fact, since it was written in the 18th century, it was a very radical document. And so if I were writing it today, I would stress that point—a very radical document. And so Beard changed his mind and his ideas, of course, everybody does if he does any thinking. Unless he stops growing, you know, at 30 or 40 years of age. Why, he will change his ideas and Beard changed his ideas. Of course, Beard made a very important contribution toward the early part of the century along with some other historians by emphasizing or introducing the economic factor in the history of the U.S. Of course, it is a very important factor, but it is not the only controlling factor[29]

In his presidential speech to the American Historical Association (AHA) on December 26, 1933, Beard gave a detailed account of his philosophy of history. He rejected von Ranke's long-accepted assertion that it is possible to describe the past as it actually was. Rather, Beard believed that "any written history inevitably reflects the thought of the author in his time and cultural setting."[30] Beard quoted Croce's statement that history is contemporary thought about the past. And he added that "it is history as thought, not as actuality, record, or specific knowledge, that is really meant when the term history is used in its widest and most general significance."[31] Beard rejected the orthodox belief that historical study follows a deterministic sequence specifically modelled on the methods of physics or biology. He did not accept a deterministic concept of cause and effect, and thus he gave sanction to the idea held by Counts that the course of events *can* be changed by human activity. The future of America is not inevitably ordained by the passage of time; we can intervene and to a certain extent mold the future according to the purposes we have in mind. In the broadest sense, social purposes can be discovered and clarified through history. Hence, Beard's rejection of the Rankian view was ballast to Counts's own form of social reconstruction.

Perhaps it should be mentioned that after Beard's death his point of view was thoroughly rejected by another president of the AHA, Samuel Eliot Morrison. In a sympathetic but critical appraisal of Beard's position, Morrison said, "The historian's professional duty is primarily to illuminate the past for his hearers or readers; only secondarily and derivatively should he be concerned with influencing the future."[32] Morrison discounted Beard's assertion that the historian had to adopt and reveal a frame of reference, and called such a selection and arrangement of facts not history but "a sort of imprecatory preaching."[33] Nevertheless, Beard's view was enormously appealing to Counts, who, like Beard, believed profoundly that the history of America was indicating that it would become a collectivist democracy.

It is not clear when Counts realized that history, used in Beard's way, could be a powerful instrument in forging his own social theory. If contemporary social forces might point toward an educational program of social action, the argument would be enormously strengthened by the selective ballast of the past. This is just what Counts needed to make his case watertight. And this is exactly how he constructed his book, *The Social Foundations of Education*, which significantly was originally to be coauthored by Beard. Perhaps of all the reasons that Beard and Counts found each other to be such agreeable persons, none was in fact more powerful than Beard's philosophy of history as it found an echo in Counts's philosophy of education. Beard's reference to Counts as "his beloved son" reflects a prophet-disciple relationship as well as genuine affection.

American Historical Association

Merle Curti has referred to Beard's generosity in reading and commenting on the work of colleagues and friends,[34] a generosity he also showed to Counts. Counts himself had the opportunity after Beard's death to pay tribute to his friend by contributing a chapter, "Charles Beard, The Public Man,"[35] to the volume of collected essays in honor of Beard edited by Howard K. Beale. (Incidentally, it was through Counts that Beale first came to Beard's attention.) No one who knew Counts, even if only through his writings, would ever doubt his admiration for Beard; it was an admiration enriched with affection. Theirs was, as their letters reveal, a "special relationship." This relationship began in 1929 when both men served as members of the Commission on the Social Studies in the Schools, which acted under the auspices of the American Historical Association.

Members of the AHA felt an urgent need in the middle 1920s to make an extensive examination of the state of the social sciences in the schools. There was some precedent for this concern, for the AHA had earlier set up special commissions. In 1896 the AHA appointed a Committee of Seven "to consider the subject of history in the secondary schools and to draw up a scheme of college entrance requirements in history."[36] The report was published in 1899 and was credited with being "the most comprehensive and thoroughgoing treatment of the subject of history in the secondary schools published in America up to that time."[37] A Committee of Five was appointed in 1907 to make modifications to the previous report in the light of criticism and changed circumstances. Its report was forthcoming in 1911. Although the report failed to satisfy the demands of both the schools and the public, it succeeded in undermining the authority of the report of the Committee of Seven. Thus the teaching of history and social science in the high school entered "a period of experiment and almost of anarchy."[38]

Meanwhile, in 1905 a Committee of Eight was appointed to consider the problems of teaching history in the elementary schools. This report was published four years later, and opened "a new era in the history work of the lower schools."[39] A second Committee of Eight was formed in 1918 to meet the demand, precipitated by the events of the First World War, that a more contemporary slant be given to the history curriculum. The committee's recommendations, which included a comprehensive course of study covering grades 1-12, were complete by April 1921. Guy Stanton Ford was one of the eight members. Henry Johnson, professor of history at Teachers College, although not a member of the committee, prepared some of the course syllabi. Johnson was also in attendance at the Conference on Social Studies in the School Curriculum held in Briarcliff, New York, on May 29-30, 1921. Edgar Dawson, Alexander T. Inglis, in whose memory the Harvard Lectures were initiated,[40] and Leon C. Marshall, who, like Johnson, later became a member of the Commission on the Social Studies, were among the ten participants.

Johnson and Dawson were also members of yet another committee sponsored by the AHA's Committee on History in the Schools and the Institute of Educational Research of Teachers College—the History Curricula Inquiry. Dawson, professor of history and social science at Hunter College, was director of the investigation. The committee published its results in the *Historical Outlook* of June 1924, and also in pamphlet form.[41] Among the resolutions presented to the AHA on December 29, 1924 by the committee's chairman, William E. Lingelbach, was that special consideration be accorded "[t]he advisability of a comprehensive survey of history and the other social studies in the schools, either by a new investigation or preferably by an extension of the survey now in progress to include associated administrative problems, the time allotment to history in comparison with that given other subjects, and like questions."[42]

Krey Appointed Chair

Lingelbach's was not an unexpected recommendation, for, at a meeting of the Executive Council of the AHA held at Columbia University in the previous November, Dawson warned that the study of history in the schools would likely be eliminated unless "a man of the first consideration from the historical association were appointed to make the struggle in behalf of history."[43] Dawson, Carlton J.H. Hayes, and Arthur M. Schlesinger were instructed "to recommend a man." On December 29, 1924 such a man was recommended and endorsed by the AHA—Professor August C. Krey of the University of Minnesota. John S. Bassett, secretary of the AHA, wrote to Krey at the end of January notifying him of his nomination and urging him to accept. Dawson, Dana Munro, second vice-president, and Guy Stanton Ford, the graduate dean at the University of Minnesota, all wrote within a few days to try to persuade the reluctant Krey to accept. His reluctance was no mere protestation. He saw clearly the magnitude of the task—saw it clearer than any of the others. Krey's commitment to any undertaking was total, and in the years between his appointment and the formation and full functioning of the commission he wrote reports, letters, and requests for funding, kept books, cajoled, persuaded, and smoothed ruffled feathers. There is little doubt that the strain of the commission's work caused his breakdown in the fall of 1933.

On February 13, 1925 Krey rather reluctantly accepted the invitation to serve as chairman of the Committee on History Teaching in the Schools, and it is doubtful if any other person could have carried out the charge so magnificently. Dawson was correct when he said, "[Y]ou are the man for the job,—young, strong, thoroughly trained, in a powerful university, within reach of a number of others, not cursed with the effete indifference of the Atlantic Coast."[44] And there is no question that Krey was anything but indifferent. Moreover, even during those periods of the commission's work when differences were apparent and tempers were running high, no criticism of Krey is found. In consultation with Bassett and Charles M. Andrews, the current president of the AHA, Krey was to appoint other members of the new committee. Dawson never was a member of the committee, but his advice was sought during the early period of its existence, and he served as assistant to Krey from January until September 1929, while on sabbatical leave from Hunter College. During the first two months of that year Dawson visited fifteen southern states collecting information for the committee. Krey later acknowledged that Dawson's efforts led directly to the investigation.

It was in this context that the committee's work was initiated. In our rush to get things done, we might these days find the process unconscionably drawn out, for, from the inception of the commission in December 1924 until the publication of its *Conclusions and Recommendations* (which was among the earlier productions), ten years elapsed. But AHA members had the experience of the former committees, and there is no doubt that they were aware that postwar conditions would necessitate an even more protracted inquiry. As it turned out, the preliminary stages alone took four years.

Krey, in a report dated November 1925, gave an extensive account of the first year's work to the AHA at its annual meeting, held this time in Ann Arbor. He estimated that the task of the committee could be accomplished within five years at the outside, although he mentioned that "[o]ne educational leader with whom I discussed the subject gave it as his opinion that 10 years would be required."[45] It was, for the last volume, *The History of Freedom of Teaching in the Schools* by Howard K. Beale, was not published until 1941, although most of the volumes appeared in the middle 1930s. Committee members were named at a meeting of the AHA's Executive Council on December 31. Bassett, Johnson, Krey, Lingelbach, and Marshall were joined by Guy Stanton Ford, Ernest Horn of the University of Iowa, Charles E. Merriam of the University of Chicago, and Jesse H. Newlon, superintendent of schools, Denver, who, in 1927, became director of the Lincoln School, Teachers College.

At the next annual meeting, held in Rochester on December 29-30, 1926, Krey still expressed the hope that the work could be completed within five years, but that was now mentioned as a minimal time. The recommendations of his Planning Committee were approved. The work was to be divided up in a form that foreshadowed the final arrangement. The committee was to examine objectives, content, teaching methods, and testing, as well as training, principally of those preparing to become teachers of history.

Immediately at the conclusion of the Rochester meetings, Krey wrote letters to a large number of"persons in the different fields concerned"[46] in an effort to elicit interest in the work of the committee. Among those who responded with "somewhat extended comment"[47] was George S. Counts.

Counts Appointed

At this time, Counts, still under the influence of Judd, was gaining a reputation as an empiricist of some ability. It had been planned that the committee would carry out work of an empirical nature—indeed by that time had already done much—and Counts possessed the appropriate skills.[48] In addition, the committee needed to be enlarged to include more educators, Ballou, Horn, and Newlon being the only three. Counts filled both gaps.

In his reply to Krey's letter sent to him after the Rochester meetings, Counts made two suggestions. First, he thought that the committee's general plan and procedure should not display too much interest "in the academic fortunes of any particular division of subject matter."[49] Second, he believed that the committee should include a review of foreign educational practice, particularly the developments in Russia and in the Folk High Schools of Denmark. Both suggestions reflected some of Counts's basic beliefs. The first he shared with other progressive educators: that the traditional division of subject matter is completely artificial and in no way reflects the conditions of life. The second, although not in any respect a unique point of view, indicated one of Counts's recurring themes: that in the modern age it is not only not desirable but not possible to examine competently any institution of society, least of all its educational system, without reference to a wider, world context. In fact, the committee hoped to undertake "careful observation of actual practice in at least France, Germany, Austria, and England."[50] As it transpired, this was not done, although it had been planned by the original committee of nine.

Counts spent the summer of that year, 1927, in Russia. It was to be the first of three trips to the Soviet Union. On his return he moved from his position at the University of Chicago, his alma mater, to become professor of education at Teachers College, and associate director of the International Institute, under Paul Monroe. Even as late as December 17, 1928, Counts had not definitely been selected as a member of the committee, for Dawson was urging his membership by writing to Krey that "everything I learn about him raises him in my estimation."[51] But Counts, along with Beard and others,[52] to a total of sixteen,[53] was nominated at the 1928 meeting of the AHA.[54]

During 1927 the Carnegie Corporation donated $15,000 to the work of the commission; an additional $50,000 was forthcoming at the end of 1928.[55] The corporation eventually spent close to half a million dollars on the project before it was completed. Appropriately, then, the full sixteen-member commission met for the first time at the office of the Board of Directors of the Carnegie Corporation at 522 Fifth Avenue, New York City, on February 16-17, 1929.[56] The show was finally on the road.

Counts was evidently pleased to have been asked to join; presumably he was one of those "young enough not only to possess maximum energy but also to be free from those numerous entanglements from which older, though otherwise qualified, persons could not shake themselves entirely."[57] Of course, he did not shake himself free, but rather worked with tremendous discipline and concentration. However, he was concerned that his planned, extended, return visit to Russia might prove a handicap for the commission, and told Krey that Krey should feel "perfectly free to select someone else"[58] in his place. His absence in 1929 posed no problem, and, save for a notation of that absence at the November meeting, it appears to have passed relatively unnoticed.

Beard Appointed

Charles Beard formally accepted his appointment the day after Counts, and wrote to Krey that he was "happy to be associated with you on this important enterprise."[59] The appointment of Beard revived his long-lapsed relationship with the AHA. He does not appear to have attended any of the annual meetings since the ones held in Cincinnati in 1916, yet at the 1930 meeting, although still absent in order to attend the meetings of the Political Science Association, he was elected second vice-president of the AHA, succeeding, as was customary, to the first vice-presidency in 1932, and the presidency in 1933.

The meeting in the office of Frederick Keppel,[60] of the Carnegie Corporation, was the first between Beard and Counts, although Beard's work and reputation were well known to Counts, even if the reverse were not so. Therefore it was a somewhat diffident Counts who, two days after the meeting, initiated the correspondence by telling Beard that he was taking the liberty of having the publisher send him a copy of his recent book, *School and Society in Chicago.*[61] This is an important book, for, although it is really the last bit of work that Counts produced that was fundamentally empirical in nature, it presages one theme that Counts continually enunciated—the evils of privilege.

It might be wise at this point to clear up some confusion that may stem from the official title of the undertaking. It began as the Committee on History Teaching in the Schools (the inclusion of the word *teaching* distinguishes it from the earlier committee that had, under Dawson's directorship, produced the *History Inquiry* and the recommendation that a further committee be formed), and by 1928 had become the Committee on History and Other Social Studies in the Schools. By the time of the first meeting in February 1929, it was called the Commission on History and the Other Social Studies in the Schools, but later that year was changed, at Jesse Steiner's behest, to the more descriptive but even more cumbersome Commission on Direction and Control for the Investigation of the Social Studies in the Schools. It ended up as the Commission on the Social Studies in the Schools. However, to avoid any confusion with the earlier committees working under the auspices of the AHA, whatever its current title, the Krey committee will be referred to as "the commission."

The commission perceived two initial tasks, and the completion of these occupied it throughout 1929. The first was to draw up membership lists for special subcommittees. By this division of labor it would, it was felt, be able not only to complete the work more quickly, but also to capitalize on the particular skills of committee members. The second task was to draw up a statement of principles by which the commission would operate. These were not to be rules, but a broad philosophic frame of reference. Prior to the second meetings of the commission, held in Washington on March 29 and 30, 1929, Beard had taken the trouble to send to Krey a list of sixteen searching questions he thought that the commission should examine.[62] These were presented verbatim to the membership.

Beard's Intellectual Leadership

In part because of his experience at Columbia University many years earlier, Beard was most sensitive, as was Counts, to the relationships between school and society and to the difficulties that responsible instruction placed upon teachers. It may well be that the vigor of Beard's approach was echoed shortly after by Counts as he began to exhort the teaching profession to take, for a change, the lead in shaping society. Beard's sixteen questions are provocative, and perhaps even more so today than they were fifty years ago. One should bear in mind, too, that these were questions seriously entertained and in the main endorsed by a committee operating under the aegis of the venerable AHA and were not those of left-wing idealogues.

1. Are we to face resolutely, with all the science and philosophy we can command, the question of objectives, not narrowly with reference to materials, methods, and technique appropriate to the schools, but broadly with reference to the whole responsibility of citizenship and to the values of civilization?
2. Are we to do the same for the public relations aspects of materials and methods of teaching social studies?
3. Are not issues 1 and 2 in reality the obverse and reverse of the same thing?
4. In other words is it worth while to consider objectives apart from the driving forces of American society which are making current history and directing our destiny?
5. If a program of social studies did not attract any social pressures would it not by that fact be so unreal as to be futile?

6. Since the fundamental laws of the land contemplate the possibility of alterations in the structure and functions of government, is it not true that even the basis of government is subject to civic discussion?

7. Since however a number of matters, such as the republican form of government, are well-settled, should civic instruction include only such matters? If so, how are they to be determined and by whom?

8. Since the issues of the current politics into which the pupils are plunged on leaving schools are largely controversial, can teachers of civics refuse to formulate them and to secure a fair presentation of them in the schools?

9. If the answer to No. 8 is in the affirmative, is the teacher of social studies then placed in the position of a social mediator between fires?

10. If so, are not the highest quality and training necessary in this field?

11. If so, who is to determine when a teacher has transgressed the limits imposed on the social mediator? The school board? The superintendent? A professional body? A mixed body?

12. Is it possible to formulate professional standards in this field, comparable to the "ethics of the bar", and apply them through technically competent agencies? In short, should there be a History Teachers Tribunal?

13. Shall we compile a list of all known pressure groups? Make an analysis of their methods? Ascertain from them officially what they want in terms of fact insertions and eliminations? State their ostensible objects?[63]

14. Shall we attempt to secure from prominent citizens a consensus of opinion on a number of our concrete propositions when formulated, with a view to securing distinguished backing for them?

15. Shall we reprint Henry Adams' Letter to History Teachers?

16. By history, do we mean political history?[64]

The modifications to these questions made by commission members were small, but important, and probably not altogether to Beard's liking. Regarding questions 1 through 6, the commission believed the answers should be "yes," with modifications to questions 4 and 6. In question 4 it was to be understood that "objectives" referred to "objectives of the social studies"; the word *American* was changed to *modern*. In question 6 the word *government* was changed to *society*. After changing the word *are* to *seem to be* in question 7, the members opined that comparatively few matters appear to be settled. Members felt that "no" was the proper answer to question 8; thus question 9 was nullified. Questions 10, 13, and 14 were answered affirmatively. In the consideration of questions 11 and 12, members felt it was neither necessary nor desirable for the commission to undertake to carry out the implied proposals. Question 15 was left in abeyance so that members could look up and read the Adams letter.[65] Finally, reflecting the views already espoused by Counts and Steiner, the commission did not want to limit history to political history, and likewise would not narrowly limit history and the social studies to government, but would make both more comprehensive.

It is clear that even this early in the commission's work, Beard was assuming intellectual leadership in the deliberations. In addition to the sixteen questions that he posed, he also listed eight topics that he felt should be thoroughly covered by the investigation. By drawing attention to these issues and by asking the sixteen questions, Beard went directly to the nub of the teacher's perennial dilemma: to what extent can teachers transgress (or transcend) the mores of the community, be it town, region, or nation? But, as Beard so pointedly had asked, "[W]ho is to determine when a teacher has transgressed the limits imposed on the social mediator?"[66]

At the third meeting of the commission, which was held in New York City at the beginning of November 1929, Beard again focused on the two broad options open to teachers of the social studies. One of them "assumes a fixed order of society into which each child is to be fitted by a dogmatic system of indoctrination. The other, exemplified in the political and social processes of England and the United States, assumes a changing world in which the child participates by creation as well as obedience."[67] Beard suggested that if the members of the commission believed that the second option was preferred, then the report of the commission should be firmly based upon it. Merriam was in accord with Beard and pointed out that the newer the political system the more direct and insistent is its policy of indoctrination with set ideologies. In America it is important to recognize and emphasize dynamic values. This was a key issue throughout the work of the commission. Members all agreed that the schools should educate for a dynamic society; the debate later centered around whether that society was heading inevitably in a specific direction (that of increased government planning and a form of collectivism) or not. Should the schools, particularly in programs of social studies, prepare students simply for change, or for specific changes appropriate for the new social order that some commission members, notably Beard and Counts, believed to be emerging? As it transpired, the majority of the commission members opted for the latter course, and thereby encountered tremendous opposition outside. Indeed, Frank Ballou, secretary to the commission and superintendent of schools, Washington, D.C., was publicly pilloried in hearings by a congressional subcommittee for participation in the formulation of the *Conclusions,* but more of that later.

The somewhat sensitive matter of committee assignments had been discussed early. By the end of the year three advisory committees had been set up: the Committee on Objectives, which included Beard and Counts, the Committee on Public Relations, which also included Counts, and the Committee on Tests. Counts was not originally to have served on the Advisory Committee on Objectives, probably because Krey did not want to overburden him, particularly with the Russian trip imminent. However, Jesse Newlon, a close personal friend of Counts as well as a colleague at Teachers College, urged Krey to include Counts on this pivotal committee. Counts himself regarded the work of this specific committee "as most important."[68]

Counts's Second Russian Trip

One recurring difficulty the commission encountered was simply that of gathering together so many people. On the whole, the accomplishments here, before the days of air travel, were amazing. Absences were few and unavoidable, for example, Counts's absence for the remainder of 1929. Counts sailed from New York for Europe in May with the intention of making a second and more prolonged visit to Russia. He left his family in Vienna and travelled alone in a Model A Ford approximately six thousand miles through the Soviet Union west of the Urals. This was a very special experience for Counts, and it colored his thinking for the rest of his life. He came to believe that a planned economy had to be an essential feature of any well-run industrial society, and that view was reinforced on his return to America early in 1930, when he saw at first hand the effects of capitalism gone amok. In a letter to his former teacher, Charles H. Judd, he made reference to the Soviet Five-Year Plan, which was begun in 1928, and added that "[i]f the plan is successful, and there is good reason for believing that it will be, it will be followed from period to period by yet more stupendous plans. Because of the great resources of the Union, this would mean that within a generation this country would be the most powerful in the world."[69] He was excited by everything he saw, the primitivism of the peasants, the industrial construction that was begun, the character of the people, warm and friendly in their innocence, the rising new cities out of the barren steppes. "It seems to me that it is quite possible that we may learn more from Russia during the next generation than from all the rest of the world. There never was before such a vast sociological laboratory."[70] What he did not see as yet was the darker side of Stalinism—that came only later.

Even though Counts may have been somewhat misled, he was correct in his assessment that the implementation of the first Five-Year Plan was a momentous event. Lionel Kochan writes:

> No words can give a just description of the scope and sacrifices and achievements of the Five Year Plan. The main emphasis was placed on the production of energy and construction material: coal, oil, steel, electricity, timber, and cement.... Another important aspect of the Plan was the training of workers to handle modern machinery. Yet a third aspect was the employment of every means of publicity to arouse popular enthusiasm for the great Plan.... The industrial side of the Five Year Plan was accompanied by a revolution just as great in agriculture. This transformed the system of individual peasant farms into a collective system of agriculture and required just as much re-education as in industry. This undertaking was as bold as it was breathtaking. Within a few years the habits of Russian peasants dating from centuries were violently destroyed and made to serve new collective aims. In some areas the opposition of the peasants led to a state of virtual civil war. It was in this way that the Bolshevik revolution can be said to have completed its first stage. By 1932, after many failures and achievements, it had shaped Russia into the Soviet Union we know today, which has earned a place as one of the great superpowers of the twentieth century.[71]

Counts's prediction to Judd was, as history confirms, accurate.

Beard, too, was absent from the commission meeting held in Chicago on December 14, for he was busy with the preparation of the manuscript of his book, *Toward Civilization*.[72] He sent Krey a one-page challenge, in which he again asked whether the goal of education is to indoctrinate the child into society as it exists or to give the child the skills to adapt to a changing world, a world in which the contingencies are unknown as much to the teacher as to the youthful learner. Of course, the answer that Beard preferred resided in the very question he posed: education, usually conservative, *should* play a critical role in shaping the future. Although Counts was not at the meeting to respond, his experiences in Russia convinced him that education should shape, even control the future. The schools, through the work of the teachers, should reconstruct society, and, indeed, they should help to build a new social order.

Early on his return, Counts wrote his first full-length book on Russia, *The Soviet Challenge to America*.[73] It opens with a chapter entitled "To Surpass America." The idea that it was even possible for Russia to attempt such a challenge drew forth a storm of criticism. Not surprisingly, Counts was branded a fellow traveller for even suggesting that a backward country, one ruled by a dictator and pledged to comradely principles, could approach the might of the United States. Counts reports that "[o]ne of the Hearst papers carried an editorial with the heading, 'George Soviet Counts.'"[74] Counts does not mention that he returned to America sporting a Trotskyish beard. Counts entered a tremendously productive period of his life, and in 1930 and 1931 found time to publish as many as four books, as well as a handful or articles, and to give several addresses. But these did not prevent him from throwing himself with vigor into the work of the commission. In fact, his contributions were so compelling that on August 1, 1931 he became its director of research, and was able to gain released time from his duties at Teachers College. But first he had to impress the members of the commission.

Beard Drafts Charter

During 1930 the burden of the commission's work, excepting the administrative work which Krey managed with great efficiency and courtliness, fell on Beard, who was formally charged at a meeting in Asheville at the end of March to prepare a statement on objectives. The task was described by Dexter Perkins, who had succeeded John Bassett as secretary of the AHA, as "of central importance."[75] This opinion was shared by all. Beard himself found the task oppressing him with its weight. He said, "I have taken it on, not because I feel competent to do it, but because somebody must and I seem to [be the] goat chosen by fate."[76] Through all the work, Beard displayed a charming diffidence as to his capabilities, and expressed the hope that with the assistance of the commission members "and many prayers, perhaps I can make the grade."[77] It was his inexperience with public school teaching that made him particularly ill-equipped. He kept calling for the assistance of "a hardboiled school man," which Merriam jokingly asked him to change to "a competent person."[78] He reverted later to the less flattering but perhaps more forceful phrase.

Franklin Bobbitt, of the School of Education at Chicago, was the hard-boiled schoolman frequently named by Beard. Bobbitt had been one of Counts's instructors for as many as four courses while Counts was a doctoral student at the University of Chicago—he achieved As in all four. As a member of the Committee on Objectives, Bobbitt was sent copies of Beard's draft statement and later a stenographic transcript of the Briarcliff sessions. He felt that the statement was too abstract; the commission should be precise about what students should be able to *do*. "Enumerate the activities of the good citizen and you enumerate the objectives of socializing education."[79] It was not that Bobbitt was critical of the work of Beard in particular and of the other social scientists on the commission in general; he saw it as their job to ferret out "the needs of the American population which their studies should be designed to serve."[80] But that was, for Bobbitt, only a first step, for it was then that the educators should step in and translate the specialized statement into activities. In his earlier letter to Krey, Bobbitt made his position absolutely clear:

> I must confess that after years of experience in *using* objectives for guidance in practical curriculum-making, I have no great faith in the practical value of general abstract virtues as educational objectives. I refer to such as will power, courage, loyalty, patriotism, attitudes, sense of responsibility, and the like. They are all good and needful things, of course; otherwise we should not have worked them up into our platitudes. . . . Let us list with as great exactitude as we can *the things the good citizen should do,* and do well; in that list we have our educational objectives. They can be stated in such flexible terms as to allow for differences in the original natures and special situations of the different children; and also to allow for continually changing conditions. The complexities of the social world provide us with no excuse for evasion.[81].

Bobbitt's position is important because it marked one point of criticism levelled at the *Conclusions,* which Beard and Counts later coauthored. Indeed, Bobbitt himself wrote an extended criticism of the *Conclusions.* At the same time, it is clear that Bobbitt himself held Beard personally and intellectually in high regard.

Max Ferrand, director of research at the Huntington Library, told Krey that the draft statement, when published, should stand as Beard's statement, and that much energy would be wasted if there had to be complete agreement among commission members as to its contents. To wait for agreement would entail certain compromises which would then "take much of the value and almost all of the snap"[82] out of Beard's formulation. When the *Charter* appeared, it did so as Beard's work.

Thus Beard's draft statement became the cornerstone of the commission's work, and eventually its first publication.[83] Several commission members sent Beard suggestions for items to be included in his manuscript. Among these was a long letter from Counts, Horn, and Newlon, which listed seven points for inclusion. All seven appeared in the *Charter,* and in some cases the exact wording was repeated. As objectives, they can hardly have been what Bobbitt had in mind.

1. Every individual born into American society, provided he is willing to engage in socially useful labor, has an inalienable right to a fair share in the property and income of the nation.
2. Every individual has the right and the obligation of labor.
3. Every individual has the right to leisure.
4. Every individual has the right to accurate and unbiased information with regard to everything that concerns him.
5. Every individual has the right and the obligation to live in democratic simplicity.
6. Every individual has the right to protection against excessive social pressure and stimulation.
7. Every individual should have the right to the fullest possible educational opportunities.[84]

The letter also echoed Bobbitt's call for specificity. "It is scarcely helpful . . . to say that the object of the teaching of the social studies is to prepare for citizenship. Unless some definite content is put into the term *citizenship*, the statement is meaningless. No one would find any fault with such a proposal simply because it lacks substance."[85]

Beard, as always, was busy on other manuscripts, but the draft statement was ready in time for the meeting of the commission which was held at Briarcliff Lodge, New York, on October 16-18. He was reluctant to attend that meeting for he had wanted to leave the members free "to say their worst good and plenty about the author and the draft." He continued, "Of course I am so deaf that they can do it without damage even if I am present."[86] Beard used a hearing aid which he turned off when he wished, particularly during tedious meetings.

The sixty-eight-page draft was mailed to Krey on September 1. Beard was, as ever, diffident, and he requested that the following statement be attached when the draft was distributed to commission members:

Mr. Beard asks me to say that this is a mere tentative draft in which an attempt is made to give some kind of a setting for the report and sketch its principles in bold outline. It does not pretend to represent his final draft either as to content or literary finish. It was done amid a great pressure of other work largely to furnish a more definite battle ground for discussion. Mr. Beard adds that on mature deliberation he is inclined to the view that as it stands it is a piece of cheese and can only be justified as a beginning. Any other members of the committee who wish to try their hands at the job will receive the grateful appreciation of their colleagues.[87]

Counts read the statement, and it impressed him "as a very strong document."[88]

Beard did attend the Briarcliff meetings, and there exists an almost complete stenographic report of the discussions. Clearly Beard dominated them, even though he said comparatively little. A vote of appreciation for the labor and the thought that Beard had expended in the preparation of the statement was passed, but, as Ernest Horn was quick to point out, it was not a note of approval for the document.

Although several relatively minor matters were brought up during the extensive discussions, there was general approval for Beard's draft. Guy Stanton Ford thought it "as sound as any ideal and . . . as satisfactory to me as anything I can conceive."[89] Henry Johnson said, "I think I got a bigger thrill out of this than any other that I can remember to have read."[90] Jesse Newlon commented, "[I]t is a basic statement, and one with which I am in almost complete agreement."[91] Frank Ballou remarked, "I think this statement of Professor Beard's is a fine statement."[92] Some believed that it might be too "philosophical," and Avery O. Craven thought it did not offer sufficient guidance to teachers facing concrete classroom situations. Harold Rugg, present by virtue of being a member of the Committee on Objectives, said, "I think Dr. Beard's paper is the first that I have been able to accept with tremendous enthusiasm and whole-hearted agreement."[93] Charles E. Merriam remarked, "I think this is an admirable statement."[94] Counts said, "[I]t isn't necessary to say that I regard very highly Dr. Beard's statement. I think it is an excellent statement."[95] Back in New York he wrote an appreciative letter to Beard, noting that his work "is of great importance to the entire teaching profession."[96] Jesse Steiner, in a letter to Krey following the Briarcliff meetings, wrote warmly of Beard's contribution: "I cannot refrain from expressing my admiration of the statement prepared by Dr. Beard. Couched in clear and vigorous language and revealing an extraordinary grasp of the entire problem at issue, the document as it stands far surpasses, as far as I know, anything of its kind that has previously been written. When Dr. Beard completes the revision as he contemplates, the Commission will have successfully accomplished a portion of its task that in the beginning seemed exceedingly difficult."[97]

Counts Makes Suggestions

At the Briarcliff meetings Counts made three suggestions that were taken up later by other commission members. These three are repeated themes in Counts's work: First, that "the school is just one institution among a great many that are playing upon the child"; second, that Beard needed to bring out more sharply "the importance of the shift from an agrarian to an industrial civilization"; and third, "the importance of focusing attention on certain . . . maladjustments and difficulties that are arising ever more acutely in this industrial civilization."[98] Jesse Newlon, as might be expected, supported Counts's suggestions, but Henry Johnson challenged Counts's assumption that the country was moving *from* an agrarian democratic society on the basis that that agrarian democracy never in fact existed. He finally conceded that there might be a change in degree, but Counts, although on this occasion he did not emphasize the point, always held that the change was one of kind and not simply one of degree. Beard agreed with this point of view, and cited his experience on the board of reconstruction of the city of Tokyo after two-thirds of the buildings and two hundred thousand people had been destroyed in the catastrophic earthquake of 1923.[99] The opportunity existed, at least theoretically, for the city to be reconstructed by taking advantage of the technology that existed in the West. Beard himself made an intensive study of other destroyed cities—Pompeii, Herculaneum, London, Solonika, San Francisco. A plan was worked out that was only partially realized because the people of Japan, most brought up in the fields and rice paddies, had no conception at that time of the possibilities offered by technology. They retained the attitudes of an earlier, agrarian order when they had long become obsolete. As Beard concluded, "[T]he whole scenery and all of the possibilities of the situation had been so completely revolutionized that their agrarian knowledge and agrarian psychology could furnish no support for it." He added, "And that is the challenge . . . of technology to pretechnological democratic ideas and information."[100] It was Newlon who succinctly observed that in this age of technology "[w]e need to invent new forms, new methods of social control."[101] Beard himself used a metaphor: "Our agrarian fathers worked within four fairly definite walls. They had been about the same for two or three thousand years, practically the same. There were changes but it was practically the same. Then suddenly your technologists just threw them all down and for the first time the human race barehanded confronted nothing short of infinity. I use that word 'infinity' advisedly. That is the precise word."[102]

Picking up on another of Counts's points that the school is but one social educational agency, the commission members expressed a very sensitive understanding of the reality they believed existed. This led Counts to propose that the statement should include a few pages on the position of the schools vis-à-vis society, and the great obstacles they face in carrying out the tasks prescribed for them, whatever they are. Counts believed that one of the great weaknesses of all educational theory is that it is built "on the assumption that the school is an almost all powerful agency." He added, "I doubt that very much, myself."[103] Rather, Counts asserted, "[W]e ought to recognize very frankly what appear to be the great limitations under which the school works."[104] Newlon was also dubious of the schools' impact in molding attitudes with reference to the big problems of society. Would the efforts of the schools to teach an enlightened point of view with reference to, for instance, nationalism, be outweighed by other environing factors? Newlon thought so, and gave the example of a business magnate of his acquaintance who told Newlon that his son had been almost "ruined" by the views of a liberal professor of economics. Newlon had replied that the young man could not have been ruined because "the point of view of that home, of his environment, outweighed the influence of the school."[105] Beard, with his gentle sense of humor, wryly added, "C.A. Beard believes we can do a little, but not too much."[106]

However, the fact that the schools only achieve a little does not mean that they achieve nothing. In spite of their concerns, all these men, Beard, Counts, and Newlon, were convinced that the schools could do something, and that belief grew out of their very clear insights into the role of the school and its position in a modern, technological society. Counts, still newly returned from Russia, had seen at firsthand what could be accomplished by schools, but he also clearly recognized that the culture of the school is but one of the"cultures" in which a young person participates.

Differences Emerge

It was during these three days of meetings at Briarcliff that some of the differences among the commission members began, ever so slightly, to surface. Of course, differing points of view had been expressed all along, but these had been handled with reserve. In the afternoon of October 17, Truman Kelley presented some of his work on testing. Now, the Committee on Testing had been working under some difficulty. Members were attempting to develop questions that tested the effectiveness of teaching in the social studies, but at this point they did not have the objectives set down by the commission, and, to a certain extent, had been working entirely in the dark. True, they were working on low-order questions, very far removed indeed from the philosophic level that distinguished the deliberations of most commission members. It is clear that Kelley's report was not greeted with much enthusiasm by several of the commission members, including Beard. The thinly disguised hostility caused Ford to state, rather bitterly, that "[t]he favorite indoor sport of this Commission is panning the Testing Committee."[107] Certainly some of Beard's comments were a little tart, but the testers had moved the discussions from consideration of "the big picture," heady and enticing stuff, to questions—such as whether there were fire engines in colonial times and the identity of Pocohontas—that seemed to bear only tangentially, if at all, on the central concerns of the commission.

Kelley had to face such comments as one by Johnson, who had "not much faith in these tests, so far as showing ability on the part of children is concerned."[108] Counts felt that the tests were "pretty artificial in character."[109] Marshall said, "I feel utterly at sea and 'woozey' headed about the whole thing. . . . It does not seem to be geared in."[110] Beard pointed out a serious limitation he believed to be inherent in tests of the sort proposed by Kelley: "[T]esting is limited to things that can be dealt with by the rational and logical process, and omits entirely from the picture the intuitive process of arriving at what is true or workable truth, now and in the future."[111] He added, "[T]hat kind of testing, to my mind is highly dubious with reference to any large intellectual operations."[112] And, of course, it was with "large intellectual operations" that most members of the commission were concerned. Even the long-suffering Krey implied that the Testing Committee was going off on a tangent of its own, and should try to connect its work with the work of the Objectives Committee. Merriam expressed "a certain alarm in a way for fear that the Objectives Committee, and the Test Committee are drifting apart."[113] In a letter to Krey written early in the following year, Merriam reiterated that he was not at all satisfied with the testing program.[114] Beard, claiming the prerogative of grey hairs, gave "a solemn warning that if we don't get together and hang together we will hang separately, all along the line on all these subdivisions of our work. We have got to give more thought."[115]

To repair this situation it was suggested that the two committees—the Testing and Objectives Committees—should meet jointly in the near future, which they did just before Christmas. Nevertheless, it was largely over the matter of tests that the most serious divisions developed within the commission. A lot of acrimony ensued for both Counts and Beard, the principal authors of the commission's summary report, who later, somewhat cavalierly, rewrote the section on tests and testing that had been submitted to them. Whether they were justified in doing so is questionable, but certainly without such "editing" there would have been a major inconsistency in the document. However, this is jumping ahead of the chronology, and in 1930 the differences were only barely apparent.

Beard's Draft Revised

It was resolved that Beard's draft should be worked over by the Committee on Objectives, of which Beard himself was the chair, and presented to the commission as soon as possible. Most commission members still viewed the draft as a statement of objectives, but it was becoming clearer that Beard, and probably most of the others, were seeing the need for a more general philosophic statement which would serve as a prelude, or, in Beard's own favored phrase, "a frame of reference," to subsequent work. This is evident in two motions, both of which were carried, that were presented on October 18, the last day of the three-day meeting at Briarcliff. Avery O. Craven first resolved "that Beard's draft be referred back to the Objectives Committee with instructions of the commission to re-work the draft into a general introduction to the whole program of the commission in such form as to give a background or framework of fundamental ideas in the social disciplines."[116] And, in an even more practical vein, a portion of the motion by Carlton Hayes suggested that Beard's statement should confront head-on the problems already faced by the commission. Thus, on Hayes's motion, the statement "will present the ideals and objectives of the social studies together with the difficulties in the way of the realization of the philosophical statement as well as the objectives and ideals."[117]

It may be useful to scour the future rather abruptly at this point, for the problem of objectives in the social sciences was not one that Beard dismissed. It took him more than three years to arrive at some resolution of the issue, with the publication of his volume for the commission (Part 7) entitled, *The Nature of the Social Sciences in Relation to Objectives of Instruction.* In his own "Foreword," Beard writes:

> [I]t seemed desirable to the Commission to have prepared a brief statement dealing with the nature of the social sciences, to form a background for the consideration of objectives in education; and I was instructed to make the survey.... If specialists in social philosophy fail to find here the grand amplitude required by the universality of the subject, they may be mollified a little by the reminder that the treatment is constricted by the requirements of the subtitle, "in relation to objectives."[118]

Beard's volume will be discussed later, but is worth pointing out here that the plan of the commission's work unfolded only gradually, and that it did not really come into focus until the middle of 1931.

The actual reworking of Beard's draft was assigned to a subcommittee consisting only of Beard and Krey; Beard, however, did the writing, and on March 22, 1931, he sent "the thrice accursed draft" to Krey. Krey was delighted with it, and administered (by mail) "smacks on both cheeks." Beard had incorporated what he could from the many suggestions made, and he felt it was the best he could do. It was mailed to members of the commission and to other involved and interested parties with the request that any criticisms or objections should be returned shortly. "If we do not hear from you in two weeks we shall assume your general approval."[119]

Two weeks went by and Beard received no reactions. This lapse occasioned one of Beard's exasperated outbursts from which he always rebounded almost immediately: "No, not a 'peep' out of any body about the draft.... Not a peep. Which confirms me in the view that this durned Commission should be adjourned and the business of writing, consolidating, and wiping up be given to one or two competent persons—amply supplied with funds & assistance. More meeting & talking in a waste of time & money."[120] A few days beyond the two-week deadline Counts responded to Beard. He thought it a splendid document both challenging and comprehensive. Counts had a major concern which Beard believed "should be noted in the revision:"[121]

> It seems to me that there is another underlying social reality which might well be brought in here and that is the institution of private property with all that this institution implies. In other words, it does

not seem to me to be sufficient to point to the dyanmic quality of our society, the dependence on science and technology, and the reliance on democratic political forms. To my mind this leaves out of the picture the most fundamental of all the realities and one which greatly effects [sic] the operation of the institutions of political democracy. In a word, many persons have contended that our society is ruled by a plutocracy. While this is an oversimplification of the facts, it contains a sufficient element of truth to make necessary its recognition in a candid statement of the underlying realities of our society.[122]

Others contacted not Beard but Krey. Boyd Bode wrote from his office at the Ohio State University, "Dr. Beard, as usual, writes brilliantly, and, to my eye, convincingly. I have come upon nothing to which I was disposed to take exception."[123] Unlike Bobbitt, Bode thought the document should be kept broad, and suggested the statement of an organizing idea, such as developing students' comprehensive social philosophy, would bind the work together. He thought that any particularizing, such as the inclusion of teaching units, would be disastrous. Merriam noted that Beard did not quite succeed in bringing together the various threads of thought that had been expressed at the Briarcliff meetings, but he was alert to the problem of diminishing returns for time spent on a document that had been thoroughly discussed and reworked—a view, as already seen, shared by Beard. So Beard pushed on, and by the end of 1931 the manuscript was ready for publication. His exasperation was understandable, for the work had gone through at least eight drafts before it was sent to the publishers. Beard suggested that Krey, as chairman of the commission, write an introduction to the book in which he would discuss briefly the work of the commission and a description of the circumstances surrounding how the book came to be put together by Beard. Krey complied, and at the beginning of February 1932 had sent a draft of the introduction of what was now entitled *Laying the Foundations in the Social Sciences*[124] to Counts. (Krey eventually wrote introductions to all sixteen books that were published under the auspices of the commission.) Counts went over the draft carefully and returned it to Krey, who was still groping for an effective title. A week later the manuscript had gone to Scribner's; the long-suffering editor, M.D. Howe, requested that Krey include some references to the fact that Scribner's was going to publish the entire series. The galley proofs were worked over by Ford, who sent them, along with several suggestions, to Krey on March 7. Krey concurred with Ford's suggestions, and, with some relief and pride, the next day he mailed the manuscript of Beard's

Charter for the Social Sciences in the Schools to Howe. Among other minor details, Krey mentioned Beard's habit of beginning sentences with adverbs or adverbial phrases, and his inconsistency in the use of commas.

Charter Published

From the printer's point of view, the Beard *Charter* presented a slight problem. Howe wanted each book in the series to be of comparable size and long enough to get a reasonably wide bookbinding. Beard's manuscript was quite short, and that shortness necessitated both large margins and a large typeface. The book went to press on March 21, and it was out by the beginning of May. Beard was delighted, and wrote the following to Krey: "The charter has come. Your introduction is sound in thought and history and beautifully done. You have put me in the modest niche as scribe for the commission, which is proper and pleases me. Now let the storm break and the critics be heard."[125]

At the outset of the *Charter*, Beard sets the boundaries of the social studies in the schools—"The necessities of scholarship, the realities of society, and the requirements of the teaching and learning process."[126] The necessities of scholarship demand a disinterested search for the truth, elusive as that may be, wherever it may lead. It is therefore inescapable that teachers will thereby run counter to "accepted maxims" and to "neat little conceptions adapted to popular consumption and pleasure."[127] In selecting materials to use in the schools out of the vast number of works written in the separate disciplines that constitute the social studies, there is no objective, infallible rule. Rather, selection is always "organized around some central philosophy of concept, faith, or assertion."[128]

Beard does not shrink from outlining what he sees as the inevitable realities in American society. First, it is a society in change. Second, it is an industrial society that rests on science and machinery. The young will grow into a world "in which rationality, planning, and intelligent co-operation will have increasing sway in domestic affairs, industry, and government."[129] Third, we have an elected form of government that depends for its operation and vitality "upon discussion, criticism, and the formulation of public opinion."[130] Thus intelligence and discrimination have to be cultivated in the young; we betray our heritage if teachers resort to dogmas and doctrine. "[I]nstruction in the schools in the United States must of necessity lay stress on the democratic process of government."[131] Fourth, America now operates on a world stage, and civic instruction must deal with this reality; "the domestic scene must be firmly fitted into the world scene."[132] Counts also hammered at this theme, and felt that it was shameful, for example, that Stalinism and its undergirdings were avoided in our schools, for the only way we can deal with the Russians sensibly is to understand them and their political system. That certainly does not suggest that we should advocate communism in the schools or agree with its philosophic basis, but we must be informed about it.

Beard asserts that formal education "must bring to a focus the fundamental national ideals bequeathed to us by time, and emerging from the fluid reality of contemporary experience."[133] Then Beard makes use of the points raised in the 1930 letter to him from Counts, Horn, and Newlon. Schools must foster good health, economic welfare with a reasonable standard of living for all, the obligation to perform useful labor, the right to leisure, full educational opportunity, equality of opportunity, the elimination of poverty through forms of managed social welfare, the right to privacy and individuality in dress, life-style and belief, and power to resist a gross materialism (or to live in democratic simplicity, as the letter writers put it), and the cultivation of a sense of beauty not tied to utility.

Beard, drawing on his life's work, recognized that the schools themselves are bounded by constraints which in large part come from the four great organizational forces in modern society: church, state, property, and labor. These are hard to resist; nevertheless, any instruction is poor "which substitutes incantation for research in its history and genuflections for thought about its underlying purposes."[134] He gives strongly worded instructions to teachers:

> They must secure for themselves a clear and realistic picture of modern society, gain insight into the central concepts of our industrial order and its culture, acquire habits of judicially examining its issue and

problems, develop the power to look with calm and untroubled eyes upon the varieties of social pressures which bear in upon them, and nourish, by wide study, their capacity for dealing justly and courageously with current modes of living.[135]

Finally, Beard elaborates on what he sees as the supreme purpose of education in the social studies—"the creation of rich and many-sided personalities." He lists the eight characteristics of such personalities: (1) they must possess information, the best and the truest that the state of the social sciences possesses; (2) they must know how to acquire knowledge and how to analyze it; (3) they must develop those habits which are essential to efficiency; (4) they must appropriate certain attitudes, such as zeal for truth, respect for the opinions of others, and faith in the power of individuals to improve themselves; (5) they must demonstrate will power and courage; (6) they must have imagination, or, as Beard puts it, "the capacity to compare, contrast, to combine and to construct";[136] (7) they must be able to cultivate esthetic appreciation, without which life is barren and barbaric; and (8) they must be inspired with the capacity for leadership and creative work, and to this end less emphasis should be placed on order and conformity and more on independence of judgment. These eight items are contained within the boundaries of the social studies that Beard defined early in the book. They also reflect a value system that Beard openly acknowledged: "Insofar as social science is truly scientific it is neutral; as taught in the schools it is and must be ethical; it must make choices and emphasize values with reference to commanding standards."[137]

There is no doubt that as a starting point, as a frame of reference, as a broad rationale for the work of the commission, the *Charter* was an inspiring statement. In the context of the *Conclusions*, however, which were to follow two years later, the lack of specificity turned out to be troublesome. Against the backdrop of Dewey's experimentalist philosophy, Beard's approach would seem appropriate: Beard is enunciating principles which reach beyond education in a particular time and place (in this case the early 1930s). But most teachers, according to some members of the commission, need more. For the time being, however, the response to the *Charter* was immediate, widespread, and almost uniformly favorable. The critics were few. The *New York Times* noted, "Professor Beard has woven into a closely knit fabric the results of the studies, discussions and personal approaches to the question of all the members of the committee, and has made of it a richly suggestive presentation of the theme."[138] Hollis Caswell, later to be president of Teachers College but then at George Peabody College, commented, "It becomes perfectly clear from this discussion that the commission has a magnificent vision of the task which instruction in the social studies should help to achieve."[139] George Coe, in a thoughtful review published in *Religious Education*, began, "Rarely, if ever, within the space of a little more than a hundred pages has so much fundamental, authoritative material upon character education ever been printed."[140] William McAndrew, erstwhile superintendent of the Chicago schools, wrote the following in the influential journal, *School and Society:*

> "A classic of educational doctrine," must be your estimate of the report of the American Historical Association's commission on social studies. Charles Beard, Hoosier, New Yorker, world citizen, historian, whither-mankinder, has drafted it. Krey, Ballou, Bowman, Counts, Day, Newlon, Horn, Comstock, Craven, Ford, Hayes, Johnson, Marshall, Merriam and Steiner are the other barons of this Magna Charta. They have been concentrating on it for seven years, working specifically on this report since 1929. They have gathered opinion from teachers, boiled it down, framed conclusions, criticized their own work, reached agreement and entrusted it to Expert Beard to clothe in fitting language. He has given it a dignity and poise suggestive of the best political classics of our history.[141]

In his review, Charles Judd, Counts's former professor at Chicago, contrasted the *Charter* with Counts's recently published *Dare the School Build a New Social Order?* He noted their similarities and differences and concluded that Beard "emerges from his discussion of the present situation with a theory of education which preserves much more of the conventional program than does the doctrine defended by Professor Counts."[142] Counts had evidently travelled a path his old mentor could not walk, a not altogether singular occurrence between former teacher and successful pupil. One of the last letters from Judd to Counts is dated October 24, 1931. It is a page in length and deals with Rollo Tryon's contractual arrangement with the commission for the production of his volume. There is no warmth in the letter and no message of goodwill. Yet it was only a few years since Counts had dedicated his book, coauthored with James C. Chapman, *Principles of Education,*[143] to C.H. Judd.

The commission, after all those years, had at last gone public, and the members had cause to congratulate themselves on making such a considerable impact on contemporary educational thought.

Beard himself, in spite of a favorable contractual agreement, transferred all the royalties from and rights to the *Charter* to the general funds of the AHA. In consequence of this action he received the following letter from Conyers Read:

> I am directed by the council of the American Historical Association to express to you the appreciation and gratitude of the Association for your generous gift of all royalties due to you from your volume entitled *The Charter for the Social Sciences in the Schools*. They realize that this is likely to be the equivalent of a downright contribution of several thousands of dollars. They welcome the opportunity to record this token of your benevolent interest in the welfare of the Association, though they recognize that it constitutes a very insignificant part of all that you have given and are giving to the advancement of those purposes to which it is dedicated.[144]

Counts Proposes a Study

At the conclusion of the Briarcliff meetings, Counts gave considerable thought to the general status of the commission, and to his
own position with respect to it. At the end of December he wrote
to Krey suggesting that he should head up a study under the
auspices of the commission and an Institute of Social Research,
which he hoped Dean William F. Russell of Teachers College would
sponsor.[145] In his "Humble Autobiography," Counts writes, "Beginning in 1931, I outlined in detail a plan for launching at Teachers
College a program entitled 'Institute of Social Research.' Dean
Russell was very much interested in the projects. . . . But we never
succeeded in getting financial support from the board of trustees."[146]
It appears that Counts intensified his efforts at the end of the
decade, when the help of Beard, Newlon, and Curti was enlisted.
The specific study was to be an empirical investigation of a midwestern community, preferably in Ohio, of around twenty or
twenty-five thousand people—a sort of extension of the Lynds'
Middletown study but with an emphasis on education. Jesse Newlon was to work closely with Counts. The Executive Committee
gave its general approval to the proposal at its meeting in Chicago
at the end of January 1931.

In the presentation of the proposal, Counts not only described
the focus of the work to be done, but also enunciated one of the
major strands of his mature thought:

> The central purpose of the study . . . would be to throw light on the
> problem of the adjustment of American education to the facts of

industrial civilization. The institutions and modes of life, fashioned under the condition of a simple agrarian culture, are being rapidly and fundamentally transformed. The day of the small and relatively self-sufficient rural community is gone forever; the day of a vast and closely integrated society is at hand; and the future is full of uncertainty. All we know for a surety is that the ruthless advance of science, machinery, and technology, which has overwhelmed the agrarian order, will continue without interruption and at an ever accelerating pace. The discovery of the functions and the responsibilities of education under these conditions is the major educational task of our generation.[147]

Counts proposed a budget of $36,000, and he intended that this study should be broken down to cover twelve areas. The list is interesting because it demonstrates quite clearly the framework of an idea that eventually, after many birth pangs, became Counts's book, *The Social Foundations of Education*. The writing of this text became a major task for both Counts and Beard over the next three years. The study itself, however, was never undertaken.

Commission's Future Discussed

Jesse Newlon, among the quieter members of the commission, was not only a supporter of his friend, George Counts, but was also, in his way, a very powerful force behind the scenes. He and Counts had tried to pull together the work of the commission and to attempt some coordination among the wide variety of points of view that were going in many interesting ways, but causing the work to become out of focus. Early in the new year of 1931, the two men identified specific areas of social and educational concern that should be covered by the commission, and hoped to join these with the best people to do the work. They proposed the publication of several volumes "dealing with the crucial problems of the social studies, all to be closely related to the philosophy that permeates the Beard document."[148] Merriam liked the proposal, and endorsed it in principle. On February 9, Newlon and Counts took the proverbial bull by the horns and made a list of possible projects for the commission to sponsor and actually named people they considered best suited to address them. Apart from members of the commission, the list included John Dewey, Lewis Mumford, Rexford Tugwell, Walter Lippmann, and William C. Bagley. Beard was to join forces with Merriam to author "Education and Clashing Economic Ideas and Systems," and Counts was to tackle "The Role of the School and Society."[149] By the middle of September this plan had been modified and considerably enlarged, but by then other important changes had been made to the structure of the commission, in which Counts himself became a major figure.

The commission met in Washington on May 7-9, 1931. On the first day Beard offered a resolution that the commission elect "a works manager" to coordinate the increasingly disparate efforts of its members. No action appears to have been taken, but Newlon continued to be exercised over the lack of coordination and the vagueness in the assignment of specific responsibilities to the members of the commission, which had been operating under Krey's chairmanship since the beginning of 1924 and which had been in full operation for well over two years. Newlon, writing to Merriam following the Washington meetings, expressed his belief that the committee structure was complicated and uncoordinated. Merriam, who, along with Beard, was probably one of the two most distinguished members of the commission, echoed Newlon's views, and said that radical and energetic changes were imperative or the work of the commission would "drift on into scenes of worse disorder and confusion than prevailed in the recent Washington session."[150] He hoped that he and Newlon would be able to move the Executive Council to accept three changes, two of which were the appointment "of a competent and vigorous executive" and an increase in the size of the Executive Committee from three to five.[151] The Executive Committee met in Chicago on June 5, and Krey, the third member of the committee, agreed to go along with the two proposals. Newlon was instructed to sound out Counts to find out if *he* would undertake to assume the role of the executive director.

Counts Appointed
Director of Research

Two aspects of Counts's recommended appointment, apart, of course, from Counts's own acquiescence, had to be worked out quickly: first, whether Counts could be released from some or all of his obligations at Teachers College, and, second, if he could, what sort of salary he would receive through the AHA. Counts wavered for several weeks, although Dean Russell urged him to accept the invitation, feeling "that the work of the Commission was very important for American education."[152] Russell himself was agreeable to any arrangement that could be worked out between Counts and the Executive Committee. Counts therefore was to be assigned one course to teach, which required that he deliver two lectures a week. The salary matter was already being settled. His annual salary during the 1930-31 year at Columbia was $12,000, excluding the obligation to teach during the summer. Thus Russell suggested that Counts be paid $15,000 per annum, of which Columbia would pay one quarter. Ford seemed to be opposed to Counts receiving a salary of such magnitude.[153] It *was* large, and contrasted with those of Rollo Tryon ($8,000) and Merle Curti ($4,500) for the same period. In fact, Counts's salary was later reduced to $13,333 because of an overall 15 percent reduction of pay for Columbia professors late in 1932. Incidentally, Counts himself suggested the reduction, because he felt that "it would not be fair for him to be treated otherwise than his colleagues, and he felt also that the saving which this would mean to the Commission might make it possible to provide for some additional work that might be required near the conclusion of the Investigation." Then Krey added in his characteristic way, "It is mighty fine of Mr. Counts to take this attitude."[154] Ernest Horn's salary was only $7,991, and his persistent testiness may have sprung in part from this and from an antipathy to Counts himself. He wrote to Ford of his concern that the educationalists had run away with the commission. In rather strong terms he stated that "the pedagogues on the committee have maneuvered the historians and other social scientists out of the picture and have gotten the power into their own hands so that the work of the Commission is really being done outside the American Historical Association and related associations."[155] Horn turned out to be one of the commission members who refused to sign the final report. It was already clear to him that Counts, who was one of the pedagogues, and Beard, who was not, were reinforcing each other's predilections.

In spite of the ease with which arrangements had been worked out with his dean, Counts still wavered for a couple more weeks. He was concerned over several matters. Most importantly, the two and a half years that work on the commission would require would interfere with his professional plans. He wondered, too, about the extent of authority and freedom of action that he would be permitted by the commission. As Newlon wrote, "[H]e is deeply interested in the project but wants to make sure that the conditions of work will be such as to ensure its effective prosecution."[156] Counts went to his rural home in Bucks County for a few days to reflect on the offer. He decided then to go to Chicago to speak with his former mentors Judd and Merriam. Later he visited New Milford to speak with Beard. After these discussions he decided to accept the offer, albeit with some misgivings. On their part, Krey and Ford were somewhat afraid that Counts "might want too free a hand for the development of his own ideas,"[157] but Beard was able to assure Krey that Counts "quite understands the constitutional limitations!"[158] As a result of these meetings Counts returned "with the feeling that he would have the hearty cooperation and support of everyone and that he could really throw himself into the work."[159] Counts accepted the invitation with the belief that he would be accorded the "opportunity to engage in a genuine creative undertaking."[160] Although he was to work under the Executive Committee and by extension under the authority of the entire commission, it was not possible to delineate precise fields of authority.

Merriam offered staunch support to Counts during this period of some indecision. "This is an extremely important undertaking," he wrote, "and I can not think of anything more useful you could engage in."[161] Although Ford, rather surprisingly, questioned the haste with which Counts was to assume his duties, Merriam sensed the urgency, for he believed the work of the commission to be "one of the significant intellectual stimuli of the time."[162] Counts rose to the challenge and responded to the confidence that had been placed in his capabilities. He was determined "to take the report out of the realm of the commonplace and make of it a challenging document, not only to teachers, but also to the American people."[163] Counts's appointment dated from August 1, 1931, although it was not until August 11 that he sent his formal acceptance to Krey. He was to have the title of Director of Research. From this point on, not only did the work of the commission begin to assume some form, but contacts between Beard and Counts became closer and more frequent.

Series Planned

On September 11 in New York City, Counts met with the five members of the newly expanded Executive Committee, which, in addition to Krey, Merriam, and Newlon, now included Ford and Edmund E. Day, who had left the University of Michigan to become the director of social sciences for the Rockefeller Foundation. Counts "outlined a program of work to cover the next two and a half years and it met with general approval."[164] Among the main items that Counts had laid down for discussion were tentative plans for the production and preparation of a number of volumes to be written under the auspices of the commission. It will be remembered that Newlon had sent Krey earlier in the year a list of topics that might be covered in such a series, as well as a list of authors, most of whom had been proposed by Counts himself. Merriam and Counts both voiced concern that the volumes might turn out to be of the typical dry-as-dust academic sort. If that actually transpired they would not be read, and the efforts of the commission would have been largely wasted. Newlon was adamant "that the Commission should seek the services of the most able men in the social sciences and in education to prepare critical and suggestive volumes dealing with the crucial problems of the social studies. . . . The Commission should not hesitate to deal with ideas. The social science teachers will carry on fairly well if they can get a vision of what to do."[165]

Merriam was not at all sure that it would be possible to discharge the obligations of the commission by producing just a single series of volumes, and consequently suggested to Counts that he consider a more comprehensive arrangement. By the time the Executive Committee met in September, Counts had prepared a list of two series of books, composed of seventeen volumes each, which he submitted to the five members.

The first in series A was, of course, to be the Beard draft statement, here called *The Purpose and Philosophy of the Social Studies*. It appears that Counts was to author volumes 2 and 4 of the same series. Volume 2 was to be titled *American Society and Civilization* (a change from the originally proposed *The Role of School and Society*), and volume 4 was to be titled *Education in the Industrial Age*. The outlines of both are extant. The former was to be in three parts, with the second part closely resembling the plan for Counts's earlier empirical proposal. The outline for the latter, also in three parts, is similar, but the concepts discussed were evidently to be more closely related to the work of the schools.

Publishing Contracts

The commission made inquiries of several publishing houses to see if they might be interested in producing the proposed volumes. Krey felt that only three publishing houses met the required criteria of wide distribution and a market already geared to the teaching profession: Houghton Mifflin, Macmillan, and Charles Scribner's. Krey described the terms offered by each in a letter to Beard. Macmillan offered an arrangement by which the commission paid for distribution of two hundred copies, and "should receive no royalty on the first 1500 copies, a 12½% royalty on the second 1500, and 15% on all over 3000." Houghton Mifflin "indicated that the terms were 10% net rather than list price," and "Scribners came right out with an offer of 15% list from the start, offered to give us 200 copies free, and agreed not to fix the price on any volume until after consultation with us."[166] Scribner's terms were clearly the most acceptable. Houghton Mifflin later offered more favorable plans but only after arrangements had been finalized with Scribner's. Scribner's also held a distinct advantage in the person of M.D. Howe, a most agreeable and knowledgeable editor, who took great personal interest in the work of the commission. Philip Knowlton of Macmillan's behaved with exemplary grace. In reply to Krey's letter notifying him that Scribner's had been selected, he congratulated him on the terms they had struck, and added, "You have done exactly what I would have done. . . . We all wish you good luck."[167]

The matter of royalties to be paid to authors was settled without much difficulty. They had contributed varying degrees of effort to their books, even, in some cases, to the extent of having, as

Counts did with his volume, parts written by assistants. In other cases the volumes represented the results of a lifelong study. The Executive Committee recommended that the authors should receive royalties ranging from 7 percent to 10 percent and that the residue would be set aside by the AHA "for continued study of teaching problems in this field."[168] In fact royalties for authors did go to 10.5 percent, which was the amount recommended by Krey for Beard, Henry Johnson, and Bessie Pierce. The AHA accordingly would receive 4.5 percent. In cases where the book had been fully underwritten by the commission, the authors received no royalty, and, as we have seen, Beard preferred, and indeed insisted, "that any royalties on the Charter shall go to the Council."[169] At the Princeton meetings, held in October, Beard reiterated the principle that anyone paid an honorarium by the commission should forego his or her royalty. The arrangement appears to have been satisfactory to all except Horn, who fussed continually about his terms, as he did about other matters.

Beard-Counts Volume

By Christmas 1931 the two volumes in which Counts was directly involved had become *American Society in an Industrial Age*, to be written jointly with Beard, and *Education in an Industrial Age*, to be written by Counts alone. With regard to the latter, some of the members thought there was a possibility of overlapping between the volume on American society, for which an educational emphasis had been suggested, and the proposed work on civic education.[170] "Inasmuch as Mr. Counts would be completely engrossed on the first of these works for some time it was deemed best to postpone consideration [of the second] until later."[171] This recommendation was made even though Counts himself had not abandoned the idea of having younger scholars perform part of the legwork (as indeed they did, although it was not of an empirical nature, as had been earlier visualized). Commission members wanted the focal point of the volume to be a chapter on education contained in an outline of the book submitted by Counts.

The development of the Counts and Beard book for the commission is intriguing and somewhat involved, and demonstrates some of the problems of collaboration. Not that there were deep differences between the two men; it was rather that a workable division of labor was hard to devise. Counts explained "that he had discussed this volume with Mr. Beard who had agreed to work upon it with him during the summer in the hope of completing the volume by next August or September. They had thought that when completed the manuscript might be submitted to Dewey for careful revision or suggestions."[172] Dewey did not read the manuscript, although Merle Curti and Sidney Hook did, as did also Dixon Ryan Fox and Lester Shippee. Fox and Shippee were both readers at Krey's suggestion.

During his first few months as director of research, Counts was trying to get under way the production of the volumes to be written for the commission. In several cases this task involved not simply making arrangements for people to be released or partly released from their academic obligations—Horn, for example—but also the provision of reasonable sums of money for secretarial help, travel, and incidental expenses. The Carnegie Corporation continued its generous contributions to the commission, so at no point does its work seem to have been hampered by a shortage of funds. Counts and Beard themselves were given $10,000 for the preparation of their volume on "American Society in an Industrial Age, with a special emphasis on education."[173]

The Executive Committee met in Chicago on December 6 and, among other things, approved the publication of the Beard solo manuscript, then called simply *Statement on Objectives*. Papers on objectives were to have been prepared by several members of the commission and were then to be incorporated into Beard's book, but even as late as the end of November 1932 none of these had been received by Beard. This may have been just as well, because Beard was bothered by the fact that some of those involved with drawing up objectives for teaching the social studies, those concerned with teaching to these objectives, and those hoping to test whether the objectives had been achieved manifested "no little confusion . . . concerning the nature of the social sciences."[174] In any case, on further reflection Beard was inclined to omit any statements on specific objectives if and when they were received.

Meanwhile, there had been some progress on the Beard-Counts book. After receipt of the Executive Committee's endorsement for the joint work, Counts let no grass grow under his feet; he forwarded a one-page table of contents and a more extensive outline to Beard on December 10, 1931. On the 24th Beard returned them both to Counts with extensive comments that give insight into Beard's own approach to historical data.

> [E]very book that is destined to put drive into facts is an *argument*. The argument may be may be [sic] subtly concealed in the facts or boldly announced. But if there is drive it is there. The facts in any large and complicated situation are selected. All the facts are not known or in the picture. Only in a small, strictly delimited, artificial area are all the facts present. For example, there are 48 states in the

Union. That is beyond argument. All aggregations of facts respecting a complicated situation are partial. Underneath lies the argument of selection (conscious or unconscious, it matters not).

. . . If I am partly right, then you must choose your argument and select your data to sustain it, but of course allowing stubborn and irreducible data to check (if necessary, blast) your argument. In other words you must choose your goal and outline it with as much firmness as you think the sophisticate public will stand and then run your gauntlet between the facts (or through the jungle of facts).

If so, then your task is not to juggle the outline around a little and to devise more ingenious titles. It is to make out for your own eyes, in words as hard as cannon balls, an argument. Decide down in the bottom of your heart what you believe to be the truest and most godlike word here and now. Make your argument outline. Arrange your topics from your present outline to fit the argument. Then, if you desire to sublimate the argument, choose the broad and general titles under which you intend to blow up the works and sketch the new battle front.[175]

At the beginning of the year Counts sent Beard a new outline, which was followed a week later by yet another. In his letter of January 7, Counts laid down his argument, which was to permeate his entire work for the remainder of his career:

My argument is a simple one. I shall contend that as a people we have received from the hand of Nature and from our European heritage practically all of the favors and advantages that ever blessed any people; that throughout the nineteenth century we held out to ourselves and to the world at large the promise of realizing what James Truslow Adams has called the "American dream"; that for one reason or another this early promise has not been realized and that something has gone rather badly askew; that if we were not to achieve a distinctly fine civilization on this continent, we had no business to take a land from the Indian who, at the time of our coming, was making a fairly sensible use of it; that the vast changes that recently have been sweeping over America and the world have so altered the terms in the equation, that we must restate the problem of life and recast the scale of values by which we are to live; that you and I and anybody else whom we can draw into the hazardous undertaking are to cast caution to the winds and tackle this job of restatement and reformulation; and, finally, that schools and teachers must shape their programs with reference to the needs outlined and accept heavy responsibilities for the satisfaction of these needs. I may add that in my judgment the facts will drive us irrevocably away from our traditional individualistic professions and in the direction of a society marked by the socialization, integration and coordination of the basic social processes. This, at least, is the way I am viewing the matter at the present juncture. Possibly you will wish to bring your heavy artillery into action at once and, as you say, blow up the whole works. If I am wrong I shall of course be delighted to have you do this. If I am not I shall want your support.[176]

Counts Goes Solo

As the weeks went by, Beard was growing more inclined to let Counts work out the book in his own way"without too much side-kicking on [his] part."[177] However, he was willing to offer as much advice as he thought helpful. Counts had proposed a chapter entitled "Sex, Family, and the Position of Woman." Beard's response is but one example of his assistance: "I am not hot about the woman chapter, but do not think that the subject is disposed of by the family business. Woman is a special creation and her place in the scheme is highly important. I just don't want to see her lost under the family title."[178] By April 23 Beard mentioned quite explicitly that he wanted the book to be Counts's own work rather than the product of cooperation. Beard would continue to help, and indeed contributed some actual manuscript for two chapters in the published version.[179] Counts, although eager for Beard's help, did not demur. Late in the year Counts, in a letter to Merriam, discussed his outline of the book, now called *Education in the Industrial Age*, and still implied that it was to be done by Beard and himself.[180] However, it was Counts who prepared the manuscript, rewriting, as he said, most of the material submitted by the "others." In October Counts sent Beard eight chapters to look over, and promised to send six more in a few days.

Four months after sending these chapters in draft form, Counts reworked them and sent Beard the revised introduction and the four chapters now constituting part 1. Beard responded with trenchant criticism of the manuscript:

I think that it is on the whole factually sound and sound in interpretation. But it is an interpretation. On the factual side, it does not, as you well know, present data and conclusions novel to informed historians. Most of your facts and conclusions are open to teachers in the better books on American history, even some taught in the schools.

. . . With most of your historical statement, I am in full accord, but I doubt whether the Commission will agree with us. Nor am I sure that the Commission, representing the Assn., has the right to attempt to fix a framework of historical and sociological thought. I have doubts here.

I have also another major criticism here. Our heritage (culture) has been taken over continuously from Europe. It is not the colonial heritage alone; it is the heritage down to the last minute of Fascism, Communism, &s. To stem too much back to American heritage would be untrue to the facts in the case.

Strictly speaking you are attempting to formulate a social philosophy. If this is to be done, then there should be a clear distinction between facts empircally [empirically] established and aspirations deliberately chosen and presented. As you are fully aware the intellectual difficulties of this enterprise are immense. When you come to what ought to be, you are in the realm of battle. However I cannot pass on that till I get the other parts of your Ms.[181]

Such a debate could not be carried on adequately by mail, and Counts joined Beard at Chapel Hill for four days from February 16. It was a working visit, and Beard records that the two of them "wrestled mightily with the spirit."[182] Counts agreed to recast his outline within the framework of the *Charter*. In effect, he was to come at the issues raised by Beard in the *Charter* from an educator's rather than from a social scientist's point of view. His book was to complement Beard's book, about which more in a moment.

Counts—and Beard understood this well—had the enormous task of dealing with *values* as well as facts—with not only laying out the relationship between schools and society, but also, at the same time, suggesting directions in which the schools should go based on analyses of this relationship. Beard realized that the commission had to deal with both value and fact, but he held that there should be clear distinctions drawn between the two. He was concerned with the looseness with which commission members were using the word *science*. He was adamant that the science and value parts of the commission's report should not become confused. This is a point that Beard tried to impress upon his readers in his own book, but he was not at all sure that it would be one that would be readily understood. Krey had unwisely asked Beard to "set forth what the several social disciplines purport to do, what they are intended to do, and what they might do if their devotees did the job right."[183] Beard's response was prompt and sharp:

> Now you are to be spanked. That is just the confusion of thinking which I believe has befuddled thought in the social sciences in the United States. It assumes that there is such a thing as "a social discipline" to be picked up like a hoe or a pot, or that social sciences are personalities with purports and intentions, and that they have a job to do right. I am convinced that a clarification of this confusion is *the one thing* that the Commission can do and ought to do, for its own good and the good of teachers. There are social scientists who think they ought to do something good, but no social science (assuming the existence of such a formalized fiction) thinks, purports, or intends good or anything else. In revising my Ms. I am asking what is a social science, with what it is concerned, and what is the nature of thought about it. I, Charles A. Beard, can have purports, intentions, and good in mind, but when I personify subjects and give them purports I am kidding myself. Social science in the U.S. is in a mess and so are the people who pretend to speak for it, and I am trying to clear up the situation.[184]

In spite of this strong statement, Beard conceded that "[t]he Commission must and will posit values,"[185] and that task fell primarily to Counts.

By the middle of July, although the title of the book was still not settled, the Counts manuscript was essentially complete. In spite of Beard's earlier criticism, which was intended to draw Counts's fire, he was delighted with the manner in which the book progressed, and of the almost final version he wrote, "[I]t is an epoch making book in Education and no mean treatise on social science."[186]

Beard's Volume

Meanwhile, Beard continued to work on his volume "on the nature of the social sciences considered in relation to objectives (and curriculum)."[187] Counts himself visited New Milford on November 1, 1932 to talk things over with Beard. Beard modestly accepted a monthly salary of $666.66 "on the basis of what a full (dry) professor of my state of decrepitude ordinarily earns in a university. . . . unless you think it too much in view of my state of decay."[188] In spite of his protestations, Beard was happy to take the new assignment, which was to begin on December 1. He would work for a while in New York, and thus he and Counts had some time to spend together.

Beard arrived in New York with his wife Mary on Thursday, December 1, raring to go. The Beards stayed at their customary haunt, the Blackstone Hotel. On December 7 Beard and Counts, together with John Dewey and Sidney Hook, had dinner at the home of John Childs, a colleague of Counts at Teachers College who was on his way to becoming the philosophical spokesman of social reconstructionism. By now Beard had in hand some statements on specific objectives by members of the commission, including one on testing by Horn, as well as some standard college texts in the social studies that Counts had assembled for him. It was during this period that his impatience with the testing movement, implied but dormant for a while, now surfaced. Beard wrote to Krey that testing "is all hokum and childish hokum, pretense, and sham."[189] Later, to Counts, Beard made even more scathing comments about the testers: "I abominate that crew of blockheads more than a communist does a Y.M.C.A [sic] secretary, but I shall hold my tongue for the sake of the Commission and its cause."[190] More soberly he wrote about testing that "it is an enemy of teaching and thinking. It is, even in Horn's hands, a mechanistic conception of all *values*."[191] Krey tried to mollify him, but the entire testing movement was among those issues over which Beard would not relent, at least not much: "Of course," Beard had written, "one cannot indict the whole outfit, but anyone who associates himself with the outfit is ipso facto suspect in the matter of intelligence. If nothing is left of the business except a check-up on definitions, then it is to laugh. No, not that, for the dammed folly is destroying the art of thinking by doing away with the necessity of ever constructing an intelligible sentence in history, economics, or politics."[192]

In spite of a bout with severe indigestion, as he called it, which kept him in bed for a few days, Beard worked with his customary intensity. "After stewing and laboring for two months,"[193] the first draft of the book was ready by the end of January 1933. Although modest as ever about his work, Beard was "convinced that some such statement on the social sciences is necessary to clear the air of many misconceptions and to meet the fundamental challenge."[194] The fundamental challenge was, he stated in a letter to all members of the commission, that "the country is in a crisis of thought as well as industry."[195]

Beard's outline, although different from the table of contents in the finished book, was close enough for its genealogy to be quite apparent, but changes continued to be made. By March 7 Beard had finalized the chapter entitled "Social Trends." He hoped to have the rest of the book completed by the end of the month, and requested to be taken off the payroll at that time. Some of the commission members thought that the draft submitted by Beard was "too philosophical" to satisfy the request of the commission for as clear a statement of the nature and contributions of the several social sciences as they had wished. Consequently, Beard was to have the summer months of June and July to revise the manuscript, and he was allotted his customary monthly salary of $666.66 to complete the work. At the end of July the manuscript had been "all turned around, changed, reduced, expanded, and refromed [reformed] in keeping with you[r] suggestions and the requirements of the Commission's job."[196]

Summary Volume Planned

While Beard and Counts were working on their respective books, they were charged by the commission to work on a summary volume for the commission. The idea of a troika originated (perhaps appropriately) with Counts at the Princeton meetings in October 1932, when it became clear that a final statement would be an essential part of the commission's work. Counts had suggested that three persons, familiar with all the problems, should "take all the materials, and then set up all the recommendations that can be made on the basis of the evidence as a working basis" for this volume.[197] This proposal was framed into a motion that was carried. A further motion named the chairman, Krey, and the director of research, Counts, to be two members of the troika. The third member was, not surprisingly, Beard, and although Krey joined Counts and Beard in this task, his breakdown later in 1933 meant that the work devolved on the other two. But Beard was well aware of the difficulties, both intellectual and political, of the task. In the middle of March he wrote the following to Krey:

> [A]ll three of us must sweat blood and tears rounding the whole business up in such a way as to bring real light and guidance to our bewildered countrymen. That means, as you say, that we must be near together this summer with all the stuff at hand and distill the quintessence of all that has been done for a constructive and positive declaration, without fear or favor, in the light of eternity, having only our problem of truth, duty, and responsibility before us.[198]

In spite of the obvious challenges, which they were aware would not win them any friends, the trio, the "Soldiers Three," as Krey called them,[199] undertook the task. Others shared their misgivings. Merriam, for instance, wrote to Counts, "I am afraid we are going to encounter very great difficulties in finding a line of action upon which the whole Committee or the preponderance of it will agree."[200] The task was undertaken in the middle of a great deal of other work. All three had their own books to prepare for the commission, and Counts, as director of research, was trying to hustle things along. On April 17 he sent out a call to all the prospective authors that their manuscripts should be available by June 30, 1933. Inevitably, they were not all prepared on time. Beard was also working on yet another book, *The Idea of National Interest,* and was, in addition, appointed as an advisor to Roosevelt's National Recovery Administration. On top of all he was the president of the AHA for 1933. The work of the commission had, as has earlier been stated, brought him back into that professional organization, but it involved his presence at the meetings, the preparation of addresses, and the inevitable committee responsibilities. One of these responsibilities was to serve as a member of the Board of Editors of the *Historical Outlook,* which was renamed *Social Studies* at the Christmas meeting held in Urbana. Beard became a member at that meeting. Also on the board were A.C. Krey and George S. Counts. The managing editor was W.G. Kimmel, who had not only been a student of Counts but was also general secretary for the commission. Beard now had the chance to speak directly to teachers.

A.C. Krey

It is hardly surprising that 1933 did not turn out to be a prolific year for Counts. His only important publication, which was published anonymously under the auspices of the American Fellowship Committee on Social and Economic Problems, was the "manifesto," referred to in a letter of February 8 to Beard, entitled *A Call to the Teachers of the Nation.* For his part "dear old Krey" threw himself into preparation of the final report of the commission, but, probably because of overwork, had a breakdown in the fall and had to seek temporary relief from his duties, including those at the University of Minnesota. He says of himself, "Mine is a queer afflication. Physically I am apparently all right, organically sound, unless my head's an organ. The prescription they have laid out for me is that I must not work, that I must take physical exercise, that is play golf everyday, weather permitting, and go to sleep very early, rest as much as possible. . . . Some days I feel very well, and when I do this whole program sounds absurd. Anyone who sees me would not regard me as a proper object of sympathy."[201]

August C. Krey, "Augie" to his friends, was born in Germany in 1887, and was brought to Milwaukee as an infant. Maxine Clapp, archivist at the University of Minnesota, wrote concerning Krey:

He took all his degrees at the University of Wisconsin. . . . Krey was an avid golfer, and regularly played in a foursome consisting of Lotus Delta Coffman [5th president of the University of Minnesota], Guy Stanton Ford, and William T. Middlebrook, comptroller and the first V.P. of Business [now finance] when that position was established. Krey, at least in his later years, became increasingly interested and involved with the Renaissance especially Florence. His book on Florence, *The City That Art*

Built,[202] is an excellent expression of this interest. His graduate students used to say that if Krey suddenly found himself on the streets of Florence during the Renaissance that he would not only recognize most of the people and call them by name, but also be able to converse with them easily and knowledgeably.[203]

Krey was a medievalist of some distinction, and also authored or coauthored other books, including a translation of *A History of Deeds Done Beyond the Sea* by William, Archbishop of Tyre,[204] about which Beard commented on receipt of a copy, "He seems a bit remote, but I have found pleasure in reading yr. acct. of him."[205] Krey also co-authored the fourth volume of the commission's series.[206] Krey was a member of the editorial boards of journals as well as of many professional organizations. He had taught at the Universities of Texas and Illinois before coming to Minneapolis in 1913. He was an ideal chairman of the commission, for he was endlessly patient, always a gentleman, thorough about details, and temperamentally suited to pouring oil on troubled waters and boosting the sagging egos of those temporarily low. Krey was a prolific and literate letter writer. He never compromised his views, was never two-faced or devious. August Krey stands almost as a model of the perfect professor, completely dedicated to his work, his institution, and his students.

With all their other obligations, the trio had little time to prepare the "formulation of Findings for Commission," which they were expected to present at a meeting to be held in Chicago in mid-October. By mid-July, while still at work on the last revision of his solo book, Counts sent Beard some draft chapters for the final volume that he and Krey had been working on.

Krey's breakdown, brought on in part "by the labor he put upon the Commission,"[207] took him out of the fray just at the time that the draft of the *Conclusions* was being shaped by Counts. Consequently, Counts and Beard had to spend almost a week together during the first part of September, forging the document into shape in readiness for the October meeting of the commission.

Conclusions *Discussed*

On September 29, the stencils for the *Conclusions* had been cut, and copies were sent to commission members on October 3, in readiness for discussions on it to be held when the entire commission met in Chicago on October 12-14. Beard and Counts, probably with Newlon, travelled together to Chicago. Krey felt well enough to attend the meetings, although he kept "out of the currents of discussion for the most part."[208] The discussions were heated; Merriam, Ford, and Day were particularly outspoken. Nothing caused more debate than the use of some inflammatory words. Horn, Merriam, and Kelley thought that the report was too hard on the testers. As Merriam wryly remarked, "You don't even give them a chance in purgatory."[209]

Two inflammatory words were singled out for discussion: *indoctrination* and *collectivism.* Merriam suggested that one could get at the collectivist idea, in fact make oneself clearer, by substituting "we must do more planning." On the other hand, other members thought these words should be used if they in fact conveyed the ideas intended by the commission. Ford, however, trenchantly noted that words should be used precisely, for "[t]he only people who are not afraid of words are those who do not think carefully."[210] Beard had thought carefully, and when pressed to define *collectivist* did so readily as "cooperative control with state facilitation or compulsion."[211] Day confessed that he viewed the whole concept of "indoctrinization" as the "festering sore" of the commission. But Counts reiterated one of his recurring themes put forth most notably in *Dare the School Build a New Social Order?* of 1932, "I can not myself conceive of an educational program that does not involve imposition on the mind [of] who is being educated." "We are," he added, "simply in a different world of discourse."[212] Later in the discussions, Counts returned to indoctrination: "The school cannot be made just a center for intellectualism. . . . If you set up a school you set up a system of social relationships and transmit certain values. A certain outlook on life. There is a system of values in anything that is done."[213] It was a central conviction of the social reconstructionists that a value-free education is simply not possible.

Edmund Day made the very nice point that, just because the country appears to be moving in the direction of the need for greater planning and centralized control, it does not follow that, even though there may be broad implications for education, these implications should be loaded largely onto the social studies curriculum. Day noted that the authors of the draft, Beard and Counts, "cite the prospect of the collectivist order and then take a jump over the program of the social studies."[214] He added that this leaves "wide open the question of the nature of the obligation of the social studies." He continued, "There is too little in this report as I see it said about the importance of tolerance of conflicting social studies and the fundamental importance of the maintenance of freedom of speech and freedom of teaching in controversial social matters. . . . It is adjustment to change that I think we want to guarantee rather than adjustment to [a] definite social prospect."[215]

Craven was not willing "to surrender to the whole idea of turning our social science courses over to this social training to get a collective mind."[216] Steiner worried that the collectivist tone of the document might trap the work of the commission into its time setting, and he agreed with Day that there is a need for "a more adequate and objective study of the social science[s] to prepare the new generation for a changing world."[217] Merriam thought that "one of the great desiderata in American social education would be an openness of minds, of more friendly discussions."[218]

There was general agreement that the document should be strong and, if possible, novel, not bland, or, as Beard said quoting Lord Salisbury, "perfectly fitting, perfectly true, perfectly meaningless."[219] Newlon was afraid that the report would be watered down in order to be understood by teachers as they are now. Without in any way belittling teachers, the distinguished geographer Isaiah Bowman hoped that the commission would translate its recommendations into practical terms for those teachers "without access to a library, without access to stimulating questions or personalities of others who are interest[ed] in revising [the] school system."[220] But Newlon felt that no document, whatever its form and content, would be of much use to the poor and "unfinished" teacher. Rather, the commission should address itself to the best-informed teachers. The task of the commission was surely, Newlon thought, to decide the basic principles upon which any program of instruction should be based. The actual assembling of materials in accord with these principles is a later and much easier task. Bessie Pierce, who wrote a volume for the commission and who was teaching American history at the University of Chicago, disagreed with Newlon and thought the commission should write for the teachers of today, as well as for the better-trained ones of tomorrow. But they were in agreement that the majority of teachers were poorly trained and ill-qualified. Merriam and Howard Beale felt that the report would go over the heads of the rank and file of the profession. Beale concluded, "[U]nless you give the teacher a suggestion about adapting his teaching to a changing social order, etc. he will react simply to do a lot of generalization. They can't see the implications in a report such as this. That's what happened to the Charter."[221] Frank Ballou said that the report "has to be written for the leading teachers whether they are numbered 10 or 10,000. . . . This report has got to be written on the highest possible level today and must look toward tomorrow. If you undertake it for 100 per cent of the teachers of today or tomorrow, it will be ineffective because a large number of teachers of today or tomorrow are neither prepared or interested in being prepared."[222]

Dear old Charlie Beard! One can imagine him turning off his hearing aid, as he would at times, but unable to resist turning it back on and entering into the debate. After an entire day of criticism of his draft, some of it dealing with content, some with wording only, he made a resolution, which was seconded by Counts, to the effect that "the Chairman constitute another 'Sub-Committee' to draw up another report for submission to the Committee that is 'relevant.'"[223] It did not come to a vote, and the next morning Beard was able to announce that his group had "decided to take the arrows out its flesh and came to the conclusion it had learned a good deal"[224] as a result of the previous day's discussion. This was a typical instance, and tells us much about Beard's endearing personality. He would frequently explode in a perfectly human fashion, but, if on reflection he felt he had overreacted, to use contemporary parlance, he would as much as say so and get on with the enterprise.

There was another real rift within the commission, and this existed between those who thought the report should be as objective as possible and those who were ready to espouse a point of view. Beard expressed himself most forcefully on this issue in a statement that reflects his strongly held philosophy of history and education:

I say that education being a form of action and policy . . . is an action of statesmanship, it is based upon some conception, fundamental conception of what this nation is like and what it is likely to become. It is an interpretation of history, nothing less than that, but of world history. It is impossible by any national process to construct an accurate objective picture of the trends in world movements. [E]very historian as a statesman has in his mind, the structure of his mind some large conception of what he wants to see the nation or the world become. It may be a large enlightened clarified frame of reference. What the statesman is to submit—alternative proposals flowing out of what their interpretation of what is becoming and if a statesman selects it defines the future. I say that is the only position that is one of the fundamental sayings of modern historical thought. Your control [You're controlled] by your frame of reference.[225]

This is precisely Counts's view of education and one shared by other social reconstructionists. Beard was providing strong grist for Counts's mill. Perhaps the most concentrated opposition to the Beard-Counts position came from the educators on the commission. Over Beard's objections and threats of resignation, the majority approved a resolution by Day that Horn and Kelley should revise the chapter on tests and testing in view of the criticism of Beard's draft that had been voiced. Their version was to be in the hands of Beard and Counts by November 15. It was a point of some contention later that they did not properly incorporate the revisions into the final draft, and it is certainly true that both Beard and Counts exhibited considerable antipathy to the testing movement. However, the subcommittee of Kelley and Horn did not submit their draft to Krey until December 15, and it was not actually distributed to members of the commission until they met on December 21. In other regards Beard and Counts did try to accommodate the differing views, but, even in face of these, they had been able substantially to sustain their own point of view.

Conclusions *Go to Press*

It took Beard a day or two after the Chicago meeting to regain his enthusiasm, and, as was his wont, with good humor he apologized to Ford for going off half-cocked at him. Beard was optimistic that "[t]hanks to the wallops we shall have a better report—I hope a powerful one."[226]

Howe received his copy of the revised version of the "Sacred Text" on November 27 and immediately sent it to press. It was retitled the *Mandate,* and proof copies were ready by December 6. In spite of the fact that Howe had the galleys, he refused to send them to print until all the changes that were required had been made. The commission met again at Princeton just before Christmas. All members expressed their opinions, and Beard moved that "the commission approve the document in principle."[227] The motion was passed, and, even though the debate continued for two full days, it is clear that all differences had not been accommodated. Beard's absence at all but the first morning session may not have been calculated, but he was obviously not in the mood to countenance further revisions. He was, in fact, sick from a cold and fever, and said, "When sickness is added to my general temperamental tension, my resistance powers are weak."[228] Horn, for one, regretted Beard's absence on the second day, and recalling the events over thirty years later, he was reported to have said that the commission had been on the verge of getting down to the basic issues and discussing them with some promise of success.[229] This is doubtful. However, Beard, forever the gentleman, apologized to Horn, saying that "his nerves were 'utterly frayed' and that he was 'worn out with work.'"[230]

Bessie L. Pierce probably summed up some of the dissident views when she wrote the following: "I fear very much that should this report with its avowed sponsorship of inculcation of collectivism in the schools be published that it would destroy much of the validity of the other work of the Commission. I am wondering if much more could be accomplished by omission of the word 'collectivism' which certainly is anathema to many Americans as well as being misunderstood by others."[231] Merriam echoed Pierce's feelings, and, although he did not object to any ideas in the document, he did want them softened, and he wanted *collectivist* out. Merriam had been among the first to receive the galleys, and he did not believe that what he saw accurately reflected the differing views of commission members. He objected to the haste with which he thought the document went to print, and pressed, vainly, for further discussions so that the remaining differences could be ironed out. But the limiting of debate had been imposed not by the commission, but by its sponsoring body, the AHA.

Commission Prorogued

At its December meetings, held in Urbana, Beard, who withdrew temporarily from the chair he held as president of the AHA, read, among others, these two resolutions:

> That (1) the executive secretary convey to the members of the commission, and especially to the chairman, A.C. Krey, the appreciation of the American Historical Association for their unselfish and indefatigable labors and to the Carnegie Corporation the renewed thanks of the Association for its generous financial support; . . . (4) in the matter of the controversy over the final report, the executive committee of the council of the American Historical Association shall act as a reviewing body, hold one or more meetings of the commission if deemed necessary, secure from members or groups of members within 60 days affirmative and dissenting opinions, hear all parties, and publish the set of opinions *seriatim* without alteration within 90 days.[232]

The resolutions were passed unanimously, but neither the secretary of the association, Conyers Read, nor Beard himself passed the association's action on to other commission members, apart from Counts, who was only given the information contained in a brief telegram from Beard.

Beard strictly interpreted the prorogation of the commission by the AHA, on his own motion; the commission was dead, it could not meet further. Moreover, Beard was afraid that further discussions would lead to a compromise document that would water down its message. He wrote to Krey, "It is not the number of signers that counts but the courage, insight, and appeal of the document." And, he added, with his customary brio, "It is better to be wrong about something great than right about a triviality."[233] However, Krey felt it wise to interpret the sixty-day time limit rather freely.

Counts did not notify other commission members of the resolution passed by the AHA; he was probably awaiting official word from Conyers Read after the wire from Beard. Counts also interpreted the "sixty days" somewhat loosely. For his part, Beard suspected that the push for a further meeting of the Executive Committee was a "backstairs manipulation" by certain commission members. But Merriam believed that if there was any "manipulation," it had been undertaken by Counts and Beard: "These two men, instead of checking each other, reinforced each other, and they wrote into the report the special views of each."[234] That view undoubtedly contains more than a germ of truth, in spite of the fact that Counts had tried very hard, with the help of other commission members, "to revise the statement so that it would meet with more general favor than had been the case at Princeton."[235] Krey told Keppel that "[n]o one worked with finer spirit than he [Counts] did"[236] to produce the revised version that was presented to the Executive Committee at its meeting in February 22. As it turned out, four members of the commission did not sign the *Conclusions.*

Official Dissent

One of the dissenters was Merriam. He did not disagree with the fundamental ideas expressed in the document, but he felt that it overemphasized "a special point of view peculiar in part to Counts and in part to Beard."[237] Although there is absolutely no evidence of animosity between the two men, Krey wrote, "I am almost tempted to believe the prediction made by one of my friends in political science at the outset of our work that it would be impossible to get the signature[s] of Merriam and Beard to the same document."[238]

Naturally, Counts was saddened that Merriam, on whom he relied heavily for support and advice during the time he served as director of research, should not have signed. He tried to get him to change his mind:

> I am particularly interested in having your approval of the document because of your wide influence in educational circles. The report is calling for many sorely needed reforms in the field of teacher training and educational thought, and I am sure that you are in sympathy with these doctrines as expounded in the statement.
>
> Is it not possible, even at this time, for you to reconsider the whole matter? I am confident myself that the best interests of American education will be served by such a course of action. And personally I am disturbed by the thought that our signatures on opposite sides of the question would suggest that we are far apart in our views. I am sure that this is not the case.[239]

Merriam was not the only one of Counts's former teachers who did not approve of the document. Another was his old major advisor, Charles Hubbard Judd, although not himself a member of the commission.

Ernest Horn refused to sign on the basis that the document represented a view quite different from his own. He wrote, "It is my conviction that the volume as it stands would do more harm than good to the cause of teaching the social studies in the school."[240] A year later Horn, at the request of W.G. Kimmel, the new editor of *Social Studies*, published a full version of his reasons for refusing to sign the *Conclusions*.[241] However, in a letter to Krey, Horn wrote, "I do not regard the second half of the report as a compromise; I regard it as a biased and misleading statement by men writing outside the field of their special competence. . . . In my judgment, the second half of this report will do more harm than all of the volumes of the Commission will do good."[242]

The cases of Day and Ballou, the other two dissenters, were quite different. Both had good political reasons for not signing, although these do not seem too apparent from their letters. Actually, Day did sign the document, but withdrew his signature at the pageproof stage. Krey was aware of Day's problems and back in January had expressed doubts that Day would sign. He wrote to Counts: "Day is, of course, in the most embarrassing situation. His connection with the General Education Board, which has sponsored so many things objected to in this document, and his connection with the Rockefeller Foundation, as well as a certain natural conservatism make the task of dealing with this report particularly difficult."[243] Nevertheless, Krey confessed that the main reason for Day's last-minute volte-face may be ascribed "primarily to his desire to support his friend Merriam, who looked rather lonesome."[244] There is some support for this view, because Merriam, on receipt of the galley proofs, wrote to Day, "I have no notion whatever of signing a document which in the light of my experience and judgment cannot be supported by me."[245] He even mentioned resigning from the commission; clearly, Merriam's decision not to sign had been brewing for some months, and he had communicated that decision to Day as early as December 9.

Ballou and Politics

By the end of March, Frank Ballou, who had served as secretary for
the commission, had decided not to sign, and, in a lengthy letter to
Newlon, he summarized his reasons:

> During the last two years I have had a growing feeling of disappoint-
> ment about the final outcome of our work. That disappointment has
> never been more keen than it is today because I do not believe that
> the final report that is before us measures up to the high standards
> which we set for ourselves or to the reasonable expectations of the
> profession that we would make a substantial, direct, and positive
> contribution to the teaching of the social studies in the public schools
> of America. This I think we do not do. We say many things in the
> report which I think should be left unsaid because they are destructive
> to no purpose.[246]

Ballou was superintendent of the Washington, D.C., schools, and
therefore not only had probably more direct contact with the
schools than any other member of the commission, but also had a
position to defend. As a superintendent, he was most vulnerable to
the whims of his board, and more vulnerable than most superintendents. He had to answer not simply to a local or even a city
school board, but to Congress itself, who appropriated the money
for the Washington public schools. Matters came to a head later—in
the spring of 1936.

The attack on Ballou was led by Representative Thomas L.
Blanton of Texas during the house debate on the 1937 Appropriations Bill. By quoting excerpts from the *Conclusions* out of context,

Blanton set out to destroy Ballou, who behaved throughout the proceedings with commendable dignity. As a prelude, these were among the opening remarks made by Blanton to the House on April 2, 1936:

> To every intelligent, unbiased, unprejudiced person who will carefully study same with an open mind, I intend in this speech through facts and incontrovertible evidence to prove beyond peradventure of a doubt that Dr. Charles A. Beard, Dr. George S. Counts, Dr. W.W. Charters, and Dr. Frank W. Ballou were the master minds who, aided by Ada Comstock, Harold O. Rugg, Carleton [sic] J.H. Hayes, and Charles E. Merriam, confederated, conspired, and worked together for 5 years in a deliberate, preconcerted plan to communize schools and colleges in the United States, and particularly the public schools of Washington, which are partly financed by the United States Government, Dr. Frank W. Ballou voluntarily and sympathetically acting as their secretary for 5 years, and at all times since collaborating with them.[247]

He continued,

> Dr. Frank W. Ballou, who had been trained in the communistic Teachers College of Columbia University and who for 5 years had acted as secretary for a commission dominated by the leading Communist professors, George S. Counts and Charles A. Beard, was determined that he would carry out the teachings of "Counts and Beard" and not allow any "ignorant majority" to hamper or in any way control his teachers.[248]

Blanton, trying to eliminate all progressive materials and personnel from the schools, did all he could to impress his hearers with Ballou's communist-by-association connections. When Ballou protested that he did not sign the final report, Blanton hammered away at Ballou's infidelity in not resigning from the commission.

> Mr. BLANTON. And yet, for 5 years, as secretary, you collaborated with him on this commission.
> Dr. BALLOU. I did not have anything to do with the selection of the commission. I refused to sign the report which was written by Dr. Beard and Dr. Counts. I refused to sign it primarily just because of such statements as you are reading to me, with which I did not agree, as to his philosophy of history.
> Mr. BLANTON. And yet you permitted your name to be published as secretary of the commission which he was serving?
> Dr. BALLOU. Yes; I was a member of the commission, and I was also

elected its secretary, and served for a period of 5 years.

Mr. BLANTON. You are aware, are you not, Dr. Ballou, that in the bulletin, Teacher Training in Service, issued by your head of the department of history of the Washington high schools, Professor Jones, your teachers have been told that every teacher's professional library should include the said final volume of report of Commission on the Social Studies entitled "Conclusions and Recommendations," which you say was prepared by Dr. Counts and Dr. Beard, instruction to that effect appearing at the top of page 3 of said bulletin?[249]

And so it went, on and on. Using a nauseating series of partial quotes, Blanton tried to pin onto Ballou not only communist party loyalties, but the insinuation of mismanagement of funds to his own advantage. This was the sort of situation to which none of the other commission members could be exposed, and if, as Counts and Beard both believed, Ballou had been weak-kneed about the problems, the official text of the hearings and of the 1937 Appropriations Committee reveal Ballou as a man of courage and intelligence. But he was vulnerable. Beard described Blanton as "an ignorant ass."[250] There is also some indication that Blanton was in cahoots with William Randolph Hearst. The Hearst issue will be taken up later, but that there was a linkage is evident from an excerpt from the *Philadelphia Record:*

> If a teacher approves of Dr. Counts (who is not a Communist but one of the nation's most distinguished educators) or of Dr. Beard (who is not a Communist but the country's ablest historian), Representative Blanton will be able to let out a Texas whoop and go for the scalp of one of his betters.
>
> It so happens that Drs. Counts and Beard have aroused Hearst's anger by exposing Hearst's attacks on civil liberties.
>
> To see these names crop up in Blanton's questionnaire tells us a lot about Hearst's relationship with Blanton—and shows how the teachers' oath has put a weapon into the hands of Hearst himself.[251]

Matters might have been made more simple if Counts had taken the advice offered by Merriam, and, indeed by Beard, to avoid words like *collective*, for they gained few friends, and gave ammunition to powerful foes. Beard warned:

> Once more, I venture to warn you against your follies. . . . you do exactly the thing which you ought not to do *unless* you want to be driven very quickly to the soap box. You use the clichés of communism. You in effect call for the abolition of capitalism and point to

the perfection of Soviet Russia. In short, who [you] put on a red coat, jump up on the ramparts and say to the American Legion, the D.A.R., and every school board in America: "Here am I, a grand Red; shoot me." Personally, I think such clichés are damned nonsense and the use of Russia irrelevant to our purposes. American ideals are enough. If not, there is no hope. Again, assuming that you are right at bottom, you simply defeat your own purpose. You swiftly prepare the way for the closure of the schools to your writings and influence. Now, mind you, I am not advising you against taking to the streets and the soap box. God may drive you there. I am merely saying that *IF* you want to work in the educational world, you must avoid clichés, keep out of uniform, and work in the historical medium. Subtlety is your only hope for victory with your magazine and your books.[252]

Beard certainly overreacted to what Counts had written and a few days later relented and added, "I was just walloping you for the good of the *long* cause."[253]

There is some reason to suppose that had the AHA not brought the deliberations to such an abrupt conclusion that all but Horn may have signed the report in spite of the inflammatory words. All four dissenters believed that one additional meeting of the commission was all that would be necessary to iron out some of the differences of opinion. This was, however, impossible in spite of the resolution of the AHA, because neither Counts nor Beard was disposed to continue to rework "the Sacred Text" indefinitely. "I do not want," writes Beard to Counts, "this damn folly drawn out till dooms day."[254]

Public Response

Several weeks prior to the publication of the *Conclusions,* an article appeared in the *New York World-Telegram* that clearly laid down the battle lines that had been drawn within the commission. The social historian, Harry Elmer Barnes, was himself favorably disposed toward the commission, even though it is difficult to discern whether or not his tongue was in his cheek when he described the *Conclusions* as "the most revolutionary and significant document in American education since the days of Horace Mann."[255] However, in another place Barnes was equally as enthusiastic and stated, "Of the work of the commission as a whole it may safely be said that it is one of the major landmarks in the history of American education as well as in the history of the social sciences in this country. It may well prove equally significant and potent in the reconstruction of American society if this is ever accomplished by rational methods and according to scientific principles."[256] Barnes apparently feared, quite without foundation, that the *Conclusions* might be suppressed because of the disagreement within the commission. He called for the quick publication of the document, for "[t]he times are calling for the radical reconstruction of social science teaching in the schools."[257] No wonder Counts thought Beard had authored the article!

Like the *Charter, Conclusions and Recommendations* is a short book (only 143 pages with the appendices), and consists of eight chapters. In the beginning the authors honor their commitment to the method of science and link the work of the commission to that of President Hoover's Research Committee on Social Trends. Chapter

2 contains the frames of reference, most of which should be obvious to readers of Beard and Counts. They write, "The frame of reference is based on a study of the past, of the present, and of trends in past and present—past and present as occurence and aspiration."[258] Reinforcing their commitment to scientific method, Beard and Counts assert, "The main function of the social sciences is the acquisition of accurate knowledge of, and informed insight into, man and society; that of social science instruction is the transmission of such knowledge and insight, with attendant skills and loyalties, to the individuals composing society."[259] Soon Beard and Counts reveal their hand: "Though it is highly important and necessary that the social sciences should seek to study man and society objectively, the Commission perceives that objective study of itself does not and cannot provide society or the individuals composing it with will, force, or purpose. Such immensely significant attributes of man as creativeness, planning, and ideals rest not on empiricism alone but also on ethical and aesthetic considerations."[260] This statement leads them to an estimate of the values at stake. These include the worth of the individual, democracy, interdependence, the end of individualism, collectivism, raising the standard of living for all, toleration at home and abroad. Counts and Beard reaffirm their underlying philosophy of education for an emerging age, no longer able to support an untrammeled individualism, which must give way to considerations of general, national, and world welfare.

There is no doubt that many educators, particularly teachers and administrators, would have been expecting some specificity with regard to materials and methods of instruction. The authors avoid this course—specifics are bound by time and places—and the book thereby lacks an immediate punch that might otherwise have gained acceptance for the whole work of the commission, even if it had been perceived as radical. As it was, teachers were urged, in selecting materials, to be guided by five principles: "the purpose of education, the powers of the child, the time allotment of the school, the life of the surrounding community, and the obligations associated with professional competence."[261] They were told that the content of the social studies should be derived from systematic bodies of knowledge contained in physical and cultural geography, economics, cultural sociology, political science, and history; that the library "should include books of reference, source materials, contemporary writings in the social sciences, current newspapers and periodicals, and the great classics of social thought";[262] that the competent teacher will strive to emulate "the methods of great thinkers and teachers of all ages";[263] that social science instruction in the schools be marked by scholarship, courage, and vision; that teaching is "a function of a rich and many-sided personality."[264]

This sort of writing may be a stimulus to the thoughtful, creative, and risk-taking teacher. It is not helpful to the poorly trained teacher preoccupied with day-to-day routine and faced with an authoritarian administration. Therefore it is not surprising that the storm within the commission turned out to be small compared with the storm that broke outside following the publication of the *Conclusions* on May 21. The very imprecision of "citizenship" which Counts had earlier condemned was one point taken up by the critics. George J. Jones, head of the department of history and social sciences in Washington, D.C., white schools, wrote, "A report of this kind glittering in generalities will be of little use to the vast majority of social science teachers in this country."[265] On the other hand, it was precisely this point that brought forth praise from John Childs, who felt that the report was particularly suited for teachers "who have the capacity, the freedom, and the courage to initiate and to think for themselves."[266] Dixon Ryan Fox wrote, "I have read the report through and think it magnificent. It is far beyond what I expected,—I think beyond anything that can be fairly expected. Certainly it will have tremendous influence and everyone of the Commission (who signs) will go down in the intellectual history of this country as a real leader."[267]

Franklin Bobbitt, who, as mentioned earlier, had been an ad hoc member on the subcommittee on objectives, reviewed the book at length for *School and Society*, and, sure enough, his first barbs were at *collectivism* and other phrases such as *the masses* and *the new order*.[268] Merriam's fears were founded. Bobbitt's was a scathing attack, which Beard was convinced (probably falsely) had been inspired by Merriam. The following spring *School and Society* published an eleven-page review by M.E. Haggerty, dean of the College of Education at the University of Minnesota. It was another strong attack; Krey described it as "[t]he most blistering criticism of our report which I have yet seen."[269] Haggerty called the *Conclusions* an "unrealistic volume that adds nothing to our knowledge about education, that fails to furnish teachers with the means of solving their own problems, and that, by its evangelistic style, perpetuates the least desirable traditions in pedagogical writing."[270] Percival W. Hutson, writing in the *Elementary School Journal*, was even less friendly: "This book is a weak conclusion to a quarter-million-dollar investigation. It is almost wholly a statement of opinion, and its style is such that the opinions are set forth as finalities. In long, involved sentences, subjective views are delivered as oracular pro-

nouncements from Olympus, and commonplaces are given pond-
orous utterance."[271] The publication of the book was greeted by
reports (not all favorable) in newspapers across the country from
Canton, Ohio, to Bend, Oregon, from Lubbock, Texas, to Modesto,
California. Childs's was by no means the only voice of support, but
attacks continued even as late as 1937, when both Counts and
Beard were brought to task in the *American Mercury*[272] for authoring
an anticapitalistic document. Beard called it "a false and libelous
article."[273] It took some time for the dust to settle.

Of course, the commission faced one of the age-old dilemmas
of educational writers—the charge of being too general on the one
hand, and of becoming quickly dated on the other. One of the
reasons that Dewey's educational writings have remained fresh and
pertinent is that he dealt more with the general principles of education in a changing society than with specific guidelines of the
"what do I do Monday?" sort. Beard and Counts, as well as others,
opted for the general. Beard himself, citing Lamartine at the Constitutional Convention, asked that something be left to Providence; it
is not necessary to dot all the "i"s. Ford quickly retorted that the
"Commission was not leaving things to Providence, but to elementary teachers, with little, training."[274] But Newlon felt that the
final volume "should be developed from a philosophical point of
view."[275] He saw clearly that their work would become "frozen" if
it were too specific; he urged that their document should "give a
setting on a broad basis and a sense of direction, leaving the way
open."[276]

Counts's Volume Published

At the same time that Beard and Counts were making the final changes to the *Conclusions*, their own books were being prepared for publication. Mimeographed copies of the manuscripts had been prepared for distribution to commission members. Counts sent an early copy of his to Sidney Hook, who was pleased with it.

> Sidney Hook went through our manuscript last evening with considerable care. After having read it over he said that he was a little disappointed in not being able to find anything wrong with it. He did make a few minor suggestions which I am incorporating into the document, but he believes that the argument is coherent and consistent from beginning to end. He thinks, moreover, that we have gone about as far in our argument as it is wise to go at the present time. All of this made me feel pretty good, because he has one of the sharpest minds in the country.[277]

Lester B. Shippee, the senior professor in American history at Minnesota, judged it "a corking piece of work."[278] Krey himself believed that Counts had proved himself "a potential historian of the first water."[279] And Jesse Newlon seemed to "think that that will be the masterpiece of the series."[280]

The genesis of the Counts book was discussed earlier. In many letters between them Counts seeks and Beard gives advice on both the form and the content of the book. The title itself underwent many changes, of which Dixon Ryan Fox's suggestion that it be called *Education Faces Industrial Society* was undoubtedly the snappiest. At the beginning of March 1934, Counts suggested to Krey that it be called simply *The Social Foundations of Education*. Krey liked it. "It is exactly descriptive and it emphasizes the fundamental character of the discussion it affords and will take its place more appropriately with that battery of volumes which becomes even more impressive with each new appearance."[281] Krey continues:

> The three that have just appeared, Bowman's, Merriam's, and Beard's, will strike more heavily into the social science audience than into education, though I imagine they will be read with interest by all teachers and by all students of education as well. Your book will link the two fields definitely, and, with the reinforcement of Curti and Newlon, should give educators all over the country a real thrill and a renewed faith in their place in the scheme of things. My vote, therefore, is very strong for THE SOCIAL FOUNDATIONS OF EDUCATION.[282]

Still Counts toyed with the idea of adding "in Industrial America," to the title, which Krey did not particularly like. The shorter title stood.

In the course of 1934 both Beard's and Counts's books were published by Scribner's as the seventh and ninth volumes, respectively, in the commission's series. Since both had received salaries through the commission, the royalties for the books reverted to the AHA. Counts's book is divided into three parts. Krey sets forth the argument on Counts's behalf: "He came to feel that contemporary activity and thought about education were insufficient to explain or even reveal the full purpose and function of the public school. . . . He undertook, therefore, to examine the development of American society from the time of its definite organization to the present."[283] Counts saw contemporary society as a technological one in the process of rapid change, particularly in its basic relationships and institutions. As he writes at the end of the book, "American society is seen to be in transition from a loosely organized to a closely integrated economy."[284] The character of contemporary society is such that the social sciences can be of great help in understanding it, for they can supply us with much needed data. In themselves the social sciences do not give direction; that has to be left to the various fields of practical endeavor, of which education is the most important. Thus, educators occupy an important position because they are necessarily "obliged to make an interpretation of contemporary history and with full recognition of all the hazards involved."[285]

Counts examines the basic forces that are operating on American culture, which, for him as for other pragmatists, are the democratic tradition, the rich, almost unparalled, natural resources of the country, and the fact of technology. Then he discusses eleven current trends, which were to show up also in Beard's volume: family, economy, communication, health, education, recreation, science, the arts, justice, government, and world relations. The last item was one of Counts's lifelong concerns. Among other notions, he pointed out that the world was, through the burgeoning growth in communication, becoming increasingly small. This was a theme he hammered away at even in old age.

In the last section of the book, Counts uses the facts he discovered earlier to outline his program of educational reform and purpose. He sees an end to the period of excessive individualism and the dawn of the age of collectivism.

> The central responsibility of public education in this situation is to bring the mentality of the American people into accord with their surroundings, to prepare them for life under profoundly altered circumstances, to encourage them to discard dispositions and maxims derived from their individualistic economy, and to re-furbish their minds with a stock of knowledges, attitudes, and ideas capable of functioning effectively and harmoniously in the new reality.[286]

As far as the place of the social sciences in education is concerned, Counts believed they should "be organized within the frame of reference provided by the ideal of a democratic collectivism."[287] He presents seven guidelines to this end. The social sciences should be used (1) to give an account of the lives of ordinary people of all times and places, culminating in the modern age in America; (2) to tell the story of the evolution of the peaceful arts and culture; (3) to trace in broad outline the development of democracy; (4) to recount the growth of industrial civilization and the emergence of an integrated economy; (5) to describe the contradictions within contemporary society (i.e., poverty and riches, privation and extravagance, nations rushing to war in the name of peace, and so on); (6) to provide youth with the tools to make critical appraisals of present-day life in terms of the democratic ideal; and (7) to introduce to the young the important proposals, programs, and philosophies that might bear on societal problems.

As usual for Counts, the organization of the curriculum and methods of teaching of this new education were of less importance than its content. He ends the book, however, with a brief look at both content and method. At heart, all instruction must be geared to the experience, powers, and interests of the learner, and then be employed to bring about widening perspectives. Counts rather easily dismisses textbooks, which may be another reason why he later declined Beard's offer to move into the textbook business. However, Counts did emphasize the importance of written materials in the home, school, and library. He urged the teaching profession to enlist "young men and women of intelligence, spirit, capacity for leadership, and devotion to the popular welfare."[288] They would be trained at "a center of liberal learning"[289] on the lines that he would later discuss with Dean William Russell. Once on the job, they would be supported by an administration whose main job would be to empower teachers not merely to promote efficiency. In sum, Counts believed that the obligation of the school was to bring into being a reconstructed society that would be in line with the collectivist character of an industrial economy.

The reviews of Counts's book were generally favorable. Willard Waller, writing in *Social Studies*, admittedly a partisan journal, stated, "In his discussion of social problems, Counts shows great interest in effecting intelligent changes in our institutions. He presents his case in an extraordinarily persuasive manner, and liberal educators everywhere might profitably adopt at least part of his technique."[290] The writer for *School and Society* called it "a book alive with courage and competence,"[291] and added that "Counts rises to inspiring heights in his portrayal of the country's need of the original spirit vitalizing the early pleas for education as the means for a generous and improving civic life." The reviewer in the *American Historical Review* commented, "While Professor Counts has not unearthed any new facts regarding the history of the United States, he has taken the most pertinent information available to scholars and has woven it into an understandable synthesis."[292]

Beard's Volume Published

Beard's book, The *Nature of the Social Studies,* or "NOSCY," as it was affectionately referred to by the inner circle of Beard, Counts, and Krey, did not suffer the labor pains that Counts's book did. Of course, by this time Beard was almost sixty years old and a veteran author, whereas the *Social Foundations of Education* was Counts's first, but by no means last, extended assay into the arena of a distinctly personal point of view. Krey, as already mentioned, wrote the preface, and when he sent Beard the first draft he expressed the hope that it would "serve as a spring-board into the refreshing pool of your wisdom, unequalled thought, and beautiful diction."[293] Beard was obviously pleased with Krey's compliments but remained ever modest, and insisted on some changes: "Since you will not let me add a note on my indebtedness to your thought and patience, I have cut out everything that savors of tribute to my alleged talents and capacities. Now, durn you AC, you must leave out all flowers and smells of flowers."[294]

Beard begins his book by comparing the natural sciences and the social sciences. He considers that the former are, for most purposes, fairly contained and delimited. The latter, however, are inclusive and extremely broad; hence selection, although important especially in an educational setting, is extremely difficult and ultimately somewhat arbitrary. Moreover, one cannot approach the social sciences with a completely objective mind, for everyone, expert or not, is part of the thing observed. The "thinker in the social sciences is colored and formed more or less by the ideas and interests which he himself brings to bear upon subjects under consideration."[295] Whereas a chemist, for example, can legitimately set parameters around his work, the social sciences necessarily overlap so that no such limits can be set for them. This does not mean that social scientists should reject scientific or empirical thought, but they must realize that they are not dealing with a bounded system and that, more important in the context of the Beard and Counts discussions, the principles developed do not "give any indication respecting any policies or actions to be based upon such findings."[296] As empirical sciences "they can present systems, trends, probabilities, and alternatives, but they cannot declare purposes or make choices."[297] Beard had already made this point to Krey. But educators can make choices, and these are made within the context of the prevailing ethos, which includes the facts revealed by the social sciences. The social sciences are also ethical because all scientists, particularly social scientists, exhibit preference in selection, arrangement, and emphasis. Thus, "they offer to mankind knowledge, thought, and a method absolutely indispensable to the construction, maintenance, and advancement of civilization."[298]

The introductory section of the book is followed by Beard's views on history, political science, economics, and sociology, placing the emphasis on method and the organization of thought. He then turns to the tasks of the AHA's commission: the teaching of the social sciences in the schools, which necessarily involves not only the matter of the social sciences as presented but also an examination of the contemporary scene. "In this way the formalism of system, so necessary to order in thought, is given concreteness and vitality."[299] Beard continues by going over, in abbreviated form, some of the areas already dealt with by Counts in his volume: technology, business, agriculture, health, family, education, communication, recreation, the arts, government, and justice. Beard also looks briefly at current trends of thought in the social sciences themselves. He summarizes the report of the President's Committee on Social Trends and also focusses on some ideas in the important book by Berle and Means, *Modern Corporation and Private Property*,[300] which he had recommended to Counts that he read. He felt that both the report and the book "all point in the direction of concerted and collective policy and action,"[301] in order "to cope competently and effectively with the collective problems of American industrial society."[302] This was to be achieved through education, particularly in the public schools. Here Beard and Counts are singing the same song.

NOSCY concludes with three chapters on objectives, and once again Beard stresses that objectives need to be stated broadly and not specifically. In fact, he holds that a scheme of objectives should "set forth a conception of the good life for the individual and a conception of the social relations deemed indispensable to the good life, at a given time and place."[303]

It is hardly surprising that Beard's book was greeted with somewhat mixed reactions on its publication. The critic for the *Saturday Review of Literature* was brutal even though he admitted that his own views on pedagogy did not only run counter to the current of the times, but were "a mark for flout, jibe, and sneer." This did not prevent him from venturing the opinion that "if the social sciences are as thin and shaky as they are described to be, their inclusion in a school curriculum might well wait until their health has picked up."[304] Harry Elmer Barnes wrote a lengthy review that was not wholly uncritical, but he said that "[t]he book is one of the most thoughtful and constructive works ever published in the history of American social theory and pedagogical perspectives."[305] Edgar B. Wesley, in the obviously partisan *Social Studies*, an organ of the AHA now edited by the reviewer, observed that "the volume stands as a great interpretation of a complete area of human affairs." He also noted that "[t]he cult of science worshippers will be disturbed, perhaps distressed, by Dr. Beard's relentless analysis of the limitations of the scientific method."[306] This was precisely one of the strongest points that Beard wanted to make—that the scientific method cannot be applied to human affairs in the same way that it can be in orthodox fields. Science can describe and predict, but it cannot be guaranteed to explain.

The remaining volumes in the commission's series came out shortly, although it was not until 1941 that the last one appeared. Conyers Read, secretary for the AHA, summed up the work of the commission in his annual report, delivered at the AHA annual meeting held in Washington on December 29, 1934:

Of the numerous activities of the Association, none has been of wider significance than the work of the commission on the social studies in the schools. That commission has now terminated its labors, the fruits of which are already apparent in the final report of the commission itself, and in the number of special studies which have already been published, and of which more are in preparation. Historians are by nature individualists, and it is well that they are so. It was not, perhaps, to be expected that in a commission composed of such distinguished members unanimity would be easy to secure. Nor would pontifical authority be claimed by the authors of the final report. But that this report will exercise a widespread and stimulating influence on the important problem with which it deals is our confident expectation. That the special studies will also be of high value is equally certain.[307]

Textbook Business

The work of the commission was complete, but Counts and Beard did not cease their collaboration and collegial association built up over the period of its existence. For one thing, Beard was planning to reenter the business of writing textbooks, and was hoping to have Counts move into it with him. In view of the fact that Beard later referred to "the text book racket," even suggesting that Counts write an article on the subject, Beard's enthusiasm for the project may seem perverse. Certainly he had considerable experience with the business, both in writing school texts and in reading them for publishers. One of his own textbooks, written in collaboration with William C. Bagley, sold, over the years, close to two million copies.[308] Possibly now he thought he could play a small part in forcing the business to become less of a racket, even though he had made his ideas all too clear:

> There are two kinds of writers of textbooks, those that write solely for money, and those who write only about ninty [ninety] per cent for money.
>
> Now, if you write a textbook just exactly as you would have it yourself, you won't make any money out of it at all, because nobody will adopt it. That is, the frame work for every maker of textbooks is already set largely by the people who have gone on before, we had theirs set by the people who went on before. . . . This is a professional confession to an outsider, what you find there is not what the man who writes for ninety per cent for money would like to have in there, but what he puts in because it is in the other books and the teachers know those facts, or pseudo-facts, and he knows that he has to put them in there, too.[309]

113

Beard's renewed interest in textbooks doubtless arose in part because membership on the commission had focussed his attention once again on education and schooling. During the progress of the commission's work, there was much talk about whether the results should include practical help for teachers. In fact, the original expectation was that there would be, but as time went by, the thinking of most of the commission members became increasingly abstract and theoretical. Nevertheless, Beard, among others, felt a real urge to develop materials for use in the schools, and to thus carry out "the letter and spirit of the Report." Earlier in his career Beard had written several textbooks which had been published by Macmillan. Philip Knowlton, senior editor at Macmillan's, tried to persuade Beard once again to write texts and other supplementary materials for the range of levels from grades 4 through 12. Beard enlisted support for the project from members of the commission, beginning with Counts and Krey, and including Isaiah Bowman. He also wanted the participation of Paul R. Hanna, a colleague of Count's who was at that time an assistant professor at Teachers College. Hanna moved to Stanford University in 1935, and was a well-known editor and author of textbooks, particularly social studies texts. Beard outlined the plan to Krey:

> The plan is: you, Counts, and I are to be an editorial board, all free and equal in rank, power, titles, honors, privileges, emoluments, &s. Most of the burden of executive details will fall on Counts and me, since we are on the spot, and you will be called upon to consider and propose plans, scrutinize plans, help select authors, and advise. No plan, book, or author will be adopted without your consent and approval. Terms and emoluments to be worked out later. Please let me knwow [know] whether you feel strong enough and willing to join us in this job. We want you and need you, for no one knows or understands the situation inside and out as well as you do.[310]

At the start Counts was enthusiastic, and anticipated that their joint endeavors would make quite an impression on the schools of the country. Krey was equally enthusiastic, and for most of the year interest grew. Beard was thinking in terms of a project lasting at least three years; he even got to the point of discussing royalties. However, rather abruptly, Counts disassociated himself with the undertaking. He did so mainly to concentrate on the production of a new educational journal, the *Social Frontier*. Beard tried for a while to keep the project alive with the help of Krey and Bowman, but to no avail. He wrote to Counts: "After we parted yesterday, a feeling of sadness came over me at the thought that you might decide that the text book business should not be allowed to tie your hands; for I should be lonesome without you and we need your indomitable and enlightened spirit. But you know the facts in the case, and personal views have nothing to do with the matter. It is an issue of the inner spirit for you. I would impose nothing on you."[311] The textbook issue was finaly wound up when Counts asked Beard himself to write an article for the *Frontier* "on the textbook rackett [sic]."[312] He did not. But Beard did contribute generously to Counts's new publication.

Social Frontier

Counts relayed the origins of his involvement in the new journal in a letter to Beard, but he also sought advice.

> Dear Uncle Charlie:
>
> A matter has come up about which I want your advice. A group of radicals in education, rather well distributed over the country, have been contemplating for some time the founding of a journal which will attack the whole educational problem from our standpoint and from the standpoint outline[d] in our report of Conclusions for the Commission. At a meeting a few days ago they voted unanimously that I accept the editorship of this journal.
>
> What do you think of this? Would it be worth the time and energy necessary? Two young men, both of them able and holding the right point of view, are prepared to give their time without compensation for three years if I will undertake the editorship. This means that all the details would be taken from my shoulders.
>
> Personally I think that such a journal might be fashioned into a very powerful instrument to do the sort of thing that we have talked about so many times. If I should undertake it I would give a great deal of time to it, preparing an article for each issue for several years. From a preliminary canvass of the field it is evident that there is much interest in such a venture. I think that we could develop a journal that would be widely read. The times moreover are ripe for an enterprise of this kind.
>
> Please let me know as soon as possible what you think. It is not necessary for me to tell you that I value your judgment above all others. A question perhaps to be considered is this—will this fit into our grand scheme about which we have talked many times?[313]

A few days later, Beard replied from California: "Have mulled over your problem. Here is my guess: If the magazine can be properly financed until the trial period is over, and you can be free from *all* irritations respecting finances and publishing details, I am of the opinion that the venture would be a good one. Certainly it would be in line with the broad front over which you and I are planning to advance. . . . So go to it, if you can get the proper easy working conditions."[314] Counts was pleased with Beard's encouragement and replied, "We are gradually getting our hands on a number of very important enterprises."[315]

The *Social Frontier* was launched under the editorship of Counts with the help of the "two young men," Mordecai Grossman and Norman Woelfel, as assistant editors. The tone of the journal was clear from the start, as William H. Kilpatrick wrote in the first issue:

> Its founding is definitely related to the new spirit of creative social inquiry which has been apparent among American educators and teachers during the past three or four years. If the hopes of its founders are to be realized, this new journal must become the expressive medium of those members of the teaching profession who believe that education has an important, even strategic, role to play in the reconstruction of American society. . . . It is the further purpose of the present organization to build up a nationally representative Board of Contributing Editors with the aim of making THE SOCIAL FRONTIER a prime medium for the development of a constructive social consciousness among educational workers.[316]

Counts himself stated that the *Frontier* was launched "to arouse teachers and others to the magnitude and gravity of the crisis facing American democracy and education."[317] In an interview with a reporter from the *New York Times*, Counts is quoted as saying with reference to the forthcoming first edition, "It will advocate the raising of American life from the level of the profit system, individualism and vested class interests to the plane of social motivation, collectivism and classlessness. . . . Particularly since The Social Frontier is interested in public education, it will place human rights above property rights."[318] This was heady stuff.

Counts filled the post of editor for three years and then handed it on to George W. Hartmann, who took over with the October 1937 issue. The journal was retitled the *Frontiers of Democracy* in 1939 when the editorship passed to William Heard Kilpatrick, and it ceased publication in 1943, at which time Counts was an associate editor.

Harold Rugg, the last editor of the journal, writes that a group of Columbia professors had been formed under the loose leadership of Kilpatrick. This group, known as the Discussion Group, was begun in 1928 and continued to meet for many years; it included Counts. Rugg states in the final issue of *Frontiers of Democracy* that "I think it was this group, more than any other single body of men, that made possible *The Social Frontier* and *Frontiers of Democracy*."[319] This statement is undoubtedly true in the intellectual sense. Their views are thoroughly reflected in both the editorials and most of the articles. In fact, they authored much of the material.

The first issue of the *Frontier* was greeted with some favorable comments. The ever-supportive Harry Elmer Barnes noted that a group of distinguished editors "have launched the most promising and realistic educational journal of our generation."[320] A writer in the *Philadelphia Teacher* said, "Teachers who are tired of professional journals which are preponderantly academic or snug in their 'God's in His heaven and all's well with the world' attitude will find *The Social Frontier* stimulating and progressive."[321] Beard was not only complimentary but also offered Counts some sage advice:

> I have read the Frontier line by line and find nothing to criticize in the way of materials or strategy. When I cannot wield my axe on a thing, it must be durned near perfect for the *purpose*. If you will keep the journal on this level, I think you can separate the sheep and the goats and gather a huge force for the broad view. Keep the view broad.
>
> Now you[r] problem will be to keep from repeating the same general ideas. This you can do by printing more concrete stuff illustrating your principles. For example, a good review of Lewis Mayers, Handbook of NRA, without any hot air, giving the hard facts of this here collectivism emergent, would be better than a ton of generalities. Stay clear of the popular clichés, such as abolishing capitalism, profit system, and private property, which merely make people see Red.
>
> Read Shapiro's [sic] new book on Condorcet.[322] Review it. That shows how great men operate in an atmosphere of censorship and tyranny, and keep out of jail. They knew that a thinker in jail was a total loss.[323]

There is no question that the journal provided a new voice in educational writing. It was anything but neutral or bland, and many sacred cows were attacked in its pages. The standard of writing was extremely high, and the editorials quite fearless. One of the early correspondents to the journal would like to have known which editor wrote which editorial. The justification for not signing the editorials was provided by Counts, who said that "[t]he un-signed articles should be taken as representing the opinions and attitudes of the editors as a group."[324] C.A. Bowers has traced the rise and fall of the *Social Frontier* most thoroughly, and has also analyzed its political posture in great detail. He had some personal communication with Norman Woelfel, whose recollections of the editorial policy can be taken as accurate: "Counts, Grossman and Woelfel determined the contents of the editorials at dinner meetings held two weeks before the journal went to press. The associate editors usually outlined the editorials and then presented them to Counts for approval. 'I can remember,' recalls Woelfel, 'no single time when Dr. Counts suggested changes.'"[325]

Beard, together with John Dewey, Merle Curti, Lewis Mumford, six others, were members of the journal's original Board of Con-tributors. The *DePauw Journal* reported a few months later that the magazine was one "of educational criticism and reconstruction" and that Charles Beard was not only a historian of note, but was also "known for his liberal tendencies."[326] Beard wrote several pieces for the *Social Frontier*, including one for the first issue—"Property and Democracy"—which was essentially a challenge to the advo-cates of the accumulation of private property. Beard states that "[c]onflicts between different classes of property owners make up the principal substance of politics."[327] One might ask, as Beard asked rhetorically, what interest this would have for teachers? It is here that Beard then enunciates a theme that recurs throughout Counts's own writings. One does not have to look to Russia, or Marx, or even Utopia to find answers to this and other such questions; they are before us, both in the writings of the country's early fathers, and also in the traditions of America. The job of the teacher, then, is to make wise selection from the choices offered: to "[b]egin at once a searching, profound, and unremitting study of the writings of the Fathers of the American Republic and to con-sider ways and means of applying to our changed conditions the principles cherished by the Fathers. This seems to be the essence of grand patriotism and social wisdom."[328] Once again, Beard and Counts are very close: If schools reflect culture rather than change it, a changed educational system can come about by revolution or by selection. In *Dare the School Build a New Social Order?* Counts makes it quite clear that the new education must select what is most worthwhile in the culture; teachers must "come to grips with the problem of creating a tradition that has roots in American soil, is in harmony with the spirit of the age, recognizes the facts of industrialism, appeals to the most profound impulses of our people, and takes into account the emergence of a world society."[329]

The last piece Beard wrote for Counts was "The Court Issue."[330] This article brought a response from Henry R. Wriston, president of Brown University,[331] who refuted Beard's apparent contention that Roosevelt would be well within his constitutional limits were he to enlarge the Supreme Court. George Hartmann asked Beard to respond to Wriston, and he did so by means of a letter, "Dr. Beard vs. President Wriston." It appeared in the November issue.[332] Beard wrote only one more article for the *Frontier*.[333]

Department of Superintendence

During the course of 1935, Beard and Counts found themselves serving on yet another commission, this one under the auspices of the Department of Superintendence of the NEA—the Commission on the Social Studies Curriculum. It did not apparently occupy much of their time, although the main task was the preparation for the department of the fourteenth yearbook, entitled *The Social Studies Curriculum*. This commission consisted of eleven men, of whom only Beard and Counts had been members of the AHA's commission. There was a connection between the two commissions, for, in the foreword of the yearbook it is stated that "[t]he preparation of this 1936 Yearbook has been influenced . . . by the productions of the Comission on the Social Studies of the American Historical Association. The several volumes of that investigation have been widely distributed and are familiar to many superintendents of schools."[334]

The 1935 meetings of the Department of Superintendence were held in February at Atlantic City. Counts and Beard were both in attendance and shared a room at the Hotel Traymore. The thirteenth yearbook was entitled *Social Change and Education*. The purpose of the book was to bridge the gap between theoretical discussions of society occasioned on the one hand by the report of President Hoover's Research Committee on Social Trends and the reports of the Commission on the Social Studies of the AHA, and on the other by the practical demands of the classroom. Counts himself reviewed this yearbook; it was not a favorable review. He felt that the diverse authorship—chapters were written by various authors—meant that the work was not only uneven, but that it espoused no consistent point of view. Not surprisingly, he praised the chapters by Childs and Newlon. In the April issue of the *Social Frontier*, an editorial, presumably by Counts, summarized the panel discussion on the yearbook. It was not complimentary to the panel chair, John W. Studebaker, U.S. commissioner for education. About Newlon, however, Counts writes, "He stood out head and shoulders above his colleagues in the department and fully established his right to be regarded as one of America's leading educational statesmen."[335] But, apart again from Childs and Newlon, Counts wryly ended by noting that "[t]he whole performance was a gross and exaggerated confirmation of the basic argument from the left."[336]

Among the speakers at the Atlantic City convention were Beard, Heywood Broun, Kilpatrick, Merriam, and Dean Russell of Teachers College. Beard hammered away at a familiar theme:

> It is our duty to give to pupils a picture of contemporary society and its trends as realistic and accurate as knowledge can make it. Let us prepare boys and girls thru information and training to take part in this order of things, to contribute to its smooth and efficient functioning, to supply the knowledge and enthusiasm required to sustain the common interest, and to contribute abilities to the maintenance of the democratic processes of government and collective adjustments.[337]

This theme is echoed by Counts in several places. Beard and Counts, as well as most members of the Commission for the Social Studies, understood that their ideals would only be realized if the status of the teaching profession were raised by a superior type of preparation that did not eschew intellectual achievement.

During this speech Beard also attempted to explain and perhaps mitigate the word *collective* that had been bandied about so much. "President Hoover called it 'associational.' The term 'cooperative' has been used to characterize it. . . . Over definitions it is not profitable to tarry long. The fact stands: We live in a society that is differentiated, integrated, centralized, and interdependent in all its parts."[338] Beard's talk obviously pleased Counts, for it was reproduced in its entirety in the April 1935 issue of the *Social Frontier*.

John Dewey Society

Beard delivered more than one speech in Atlantic City that week. On Sunday, February 24, the day before the meetings of the Department of Superintendence formally opened, an unofficial program was arranged under the auspices of the *Social Frontier*. The program was advertised around the title "Steps Forward in Education." Beard, Counts, Broun, and Louis M. Hacker were to discuss the future of education from the perspective of the reports of the AHA's Commission on the Social Sciences. At least that was the advertised version of the meetings to be held that afternoon. However, during the morning an as-yet-unnamed society was organized, whose purpose was to study education, particularly in its social relations. For this occasion, they called themselves "The Conference on Education and Economic Reconstruction." The conveners were Counts, Newlon, and Harold Rugg.

The seeds for this new society had really been planted a year earlier at the Cleveland meetings of the Department of Superintendence, and the early moves were made by Henry Harap, of Western Reserve University, and Paul R. Hanna, both of whom persuaded Newlon to call a meeting of educational liberals. A luncheon was arranged on February 25, 1934. Counts had been among those invited to the luncheon, but there is no record either of who actually attended or what transpired. It was clearly seen as a promising beginning, and a further meeting was arranged, which, after some delay, was held in New York City on October 6 and 7, 1934. Again Counts was invited.

The new society, officially formed at Atlantic City in 1935, was chaired by Kilpatrick; the board included Counts and Newlon. Beard and Dewey were among the fellows of the new organization. It was reported in the *Social Frontier*, which became more or less the mouthpiece of the group, that the society "will encourage in every way possible and will itself conduct scholarly and scientific investigations of the relations of school and society, with particular reference to the place and function of education in the process of social change. Among its major activities will be the preparation and publication of a yearbook."[339] And in 1937 the first yearbook appeared.[340] The official title of the organization, bestowed on it sometime between the meeting in Atlantic City and the one a year later in St. Louis, was the *John Dewey Society*.[341]

William Randolph Hearst

On February 24, 1935, there was an invited audience of around two hundred for the morning meeting of those educational liberals. The publicized afternoon meeting that Sunday in Atlantic City attracted around nine hundred people. It does not appear that the commission's reports were discussed explicitly; rather the discussions and speeches centered around the topic of academic freedom. Beard brought the crowd to its feet in a damning indictment of William Randolph Hearst. Said Beard, "I have never found one single person, who for talents and character commands the respect of the American people, who has not agreed with me that William Randolph Hearst has pandered to depraved tastes and has been an enemy of everything that is noblest and best in our American tradition."[342] Newlon recalled that Beard's excoriation of Hearst "will be remembered as long as anyone is interested in the social history of this period."[343] Beard enunciated the need of introducing the discussion of controversial questions into the schools. "How can we do otherwise," he asked, "if we teach truth? Parents must come to understand that this is part of the function of the teacher of the social studies. Some people, I am told, don't want this kind of teaching, among them William Randolph Hearst."[344] Hearst retaliated by printing a false report in the *New York American*.[345] It attributed to Willard Givens, the newly apointed secretary of the NEA, a sharp criticism of the left-wing educators and an eulogy of Hearst as benefactor to education. Givens issued an immediate denial. The reaction of the Department of Superintendence was as "innocuous" and "milk-and-water" as the frontiersmen expected. The Resolution

Committee of the department proposed the following resolution: "We reaffirm our unqualified belief in the principle of academic freedom for all workers in education, and favor the active cooperation of the Department of Superintendence with the National Education Association in the study of the problems of academic freedom."[346] Counts's comment on the resolution was scathing: "It affirms loyalty to the principle, and then straightway retreats to a position of complete safety, quite out of range of even stray and eccentric bullets. Clearly academic freedom today is a matter, not only for study, but also for action."[347] This nonaction was particularly odious to Counts because it was not one of the so-called radicals who had been lied about by Hearst but actually the chief officer of the department's parent association, the NEA. What Counts does not mention, however, possibly because it makes the matter even more shameful, is that the superintendent of the Shaker Heights, Ohio, schools, Frederick H. Bair, who had done some work for the Commission on the Social Studies, moved a strongly worded resolution that was actually voted down in favor of the milksop one that offended Counts so heartily.

Anyway, a strong response to the Hearst tactics was forthcoming. Heywood Broun, one of the last speakers at the convention, took the offensive. At the outset of his speech he told the audience that he had been so shocked by the action taken at the morning session that he tore up his original speech and was going to address the issue that had been sidestepped by the department. He began by saying he intended to be rude. Broun did not mince words:

> I sat and listened to the Resolutions Committee come in with its report on academic freedom and the Resolutions Comittee said in effect that they had thought of not bringing anything on academic freedom at all and they only added it as an afterthought because they felt it might be dangerous. They felt it might be dangerous because they would be put in the position of defending certain teachers and professors who had gone back to Moscow. I wonder whether the superintendents of the schools have the nerve to go back to the Declaration of Independence.
>
> I wonder whether it means anything when a body says, "We believe in academic freedom, but we will set up no machinery whatsoever to fight for it." When a man says, "I believe in something but I will not fight for it," I challenge his belief.
>
> I applaud those men in the schools and colleges who are called the radical group. We have had from the beginning of America a sufficient radicalism of our own from our forefathers which we should

keep alive and defend today. This convention has been afraid of mentioning even the name of William Randolph Hearst. This convention has said in effect that if Mr. William Randolph Hearst attacks a professor, that is news; if a professor attacks William Randolph Hearst, that is not news. This convention will say nothing about it and the great press associations of this country will say nothing about it, either.[348]

Broun then said that education, as the search for truth, must inevitably be the enemy of propaganda from wherever it comes. No one in America needs to be watched more closely than the lords of the press, who are usually lords of a lot more as well:

> I do not fear the man on horseback, but I do fear the man behind a flat topped desk who can reach out and push a button and say, "Let's have a war with Mexico," and start going those forces of the radio, the press, the pulpit, and the screen which make wars possible. . . . Wars are not possible unless you have those front line troops, those people who come before the cavalry, the airplanes, the infantry, and the tanks. That is the liars' division, the people who come running, walking, crawling on their bellies, to make all things possible for the next war.[349]

Education, one that shows people the full scope of the world and then lets them choose, is a dangerous business, and Hearst knew this well.

Counts himself had been the personal mark of Hearst's tactics, the intent of which was to discredit certain professors who were known to have liberal leanings; they were to be painted red. Some Hearst reporters were sent incognito to selected university campuses to entrap these professors. The first incident happened at Syracuse University on November 22, 1934. A week later Sidney Hook, of New York University, was approached. On December 14 the target was Columbia University:

> Dr. George S. Counts . . . received a letter from a young man who said he was desirous of enrolling in order to learn "the real stuff about socialism, communism and capitalism." Counts, having heard of the Syracuse case, was on his guard. He had a stenographer with him when the young man arrived, and soon got him to admit that he was a Hearst reporter. According to Counts, the reporter said, "Mr. Hearst is engaged at present in conducting a Red scare. . . . You realize of course that because of my assignment I will have to select the most sensational statements from the interview in order to make out a good case. That is what Mr. Hearst is expecting."[350]

The reporter also interviewed Kilpatrick and another interviewed Newlon.

As a result of the subterfuges, just before Christmas 1934, a group of educators appealed to the McCormack-Dickstein Committee on unAmerican Activities to extend its investigations to a "most insidious and unAmerican attack upon our educational institutions."[351] Counts was reported to say, "If Wiliam Randolph Hearst succeeds in his efforts, he will reduce American universities and schools to the ignominious condition of the German schools and universities under Hitler."[352] A telegraph was sent to the committee which was signed by twenty educators, including both Beard and Counts as well as Dewey and Kilpatrick. It read as follows:

> Recent occurrences at Syracuse University and Columbia University indicate that a campaign of terriorism against teachers in American colleges, universities, schools and even private schools is getting under way. Such repressive efforts are not only directly contrary to Amercian democratic tradition, but if successful would make it impossible for schools to do their proper work.
>
> In a time like this we need every help in getting the people to face the serious problems confronting us. Neither cure of depression nor furthering of the progressive measures of the national administration can go forward without free discussion and inquiry in the universities and schools. This campaign threatens both.[353]

The reactions from the universities was immediate and powerful. At many of the leading schools, including not only Columbia and New York University, but also Princeton, Yale, and Northwestern, among others, students voted a boycott of Hearst magazines and newspapers. Hearst carried out such tactics on the pretext of national loyalty, but in fact his opposition to communism was also colored by his sympathy with fascism. He had been a guest of Hitler and was an admirer of Mussolini. Hermann Goering wrote several articles for the Hearst press. Heywood Broun's comments were not, then, exactly out of place.

Counts carried his battle into Madison Square Garden and on April 3, 1935 spoke to an audience that was estimated at between fifteen thousand and seventeen thousand people. The platform was decorated with cardboard effigies of the "red-baiters," among them needless to say, one of Hearst. These were auctioned off after the meeting. The purpose of the meeting was to protest the gag-laws, the various alien and sedition bills, that were pending before Congress and also a number of state legislatures. Counts named Hearst as "the most active agent of the 'reaction toward barbarism.'"[354]

Booing and handclapping from the vast audience greeted Counts's assertion that the archreactionary and symbol of this campagin to stifle free speech was "America's Public Enemy No. 1, William Randolph Hearst." Counts added "his opinion that the 'Hearst press is one of the most dangerous forces in bringing war and Fascism to this country.' He urged his listeners to picket Hearst publication plants throughout the country."[355]

Counts's *Social Frontier* devoted an entire issue to freedom of the press, and concentrated its attacks on the threats to that freedom coming by way of William Randolph Hearst. This issue is an extraordinarily outspoken document. The opening editorial, unsigned as always but probably by Counts, gives three reasons for such concerted opposition to Hearst. First, no attack upon freedom of teaching should pass unnoticed; second, the attack demonstrates the alignment of forces of society and indicates "to teachers who their probable friends and enemies are";[356] and third, it brings into focus the position of the press as an educational and cultural agency. Hearst's career was mercilessly examined by Lawrence Martin and Ferdinand Lundberg. Perhaps most interesting of all are the verbatim conversations between the Hearst reporter, identified as Mr. X, and Counts and Kilpatrick. In this same issue, in one of his regular columns, John Dewey stressed that all efforts to intimidate teachers must be fought in order to preserve the freedom of inquiry. The press and radio can be powerful forces in inculcating mass prejudice, as is apparent in fascist countries; they can only be countered by the development of a popular intelligence that is critically discriminating.

Academic Freedom

Beard and Counts were also together at the 1936 meetings of the Department of Superintendence, held this time in St. Louis. The theme of the convention was right up their alley—"The Function of the Schools in a Democracy." The central issue was again academic freedom, and, in his opening address, Glenn Frank, president of the University of Wisconsin, deplored indoctrination from either the right or the left, but seemed somehow to support it from the middle. Frank was no admirer of Counts; he was reported as saying that he would not care to head a university in which a controlling voice was had by either Hearst or Counts.

Both Beard and Counts appeared on a panel discussion on the morning of February 25, the purpose of which was to discuss the 1936 yearbook. Just prior to the panel, Beard himself delivered a paper, "The Scholar in an Age of Conflicts." He was concerned about the always present, but in 1936 particularly apparent, threat to teachers as they explore controversial issues. Beard urged teachers to take a stand on seven points, of which the following were the first and last:

> To draft a national code of good practise for the teaching of subjects which in their nature involve or touch upon controversial questions—a code incorporating the fundamental liberties of press, speech, and religious worship guaranteed by our constitutions.
> ... To establish a national body, perhaps connected with the National Education Association, provided with funds and competent legal talent and charged with the duty of promoting and defending the rights of

free scientific inquiry before the public in general and in particular communities beset by witchburners and fanatics.[357]

It is perhaps not inappropriate that the photograph of Beard accompanying the report in the *St. Louis Post-Dispatch* of his speech runs alongside a report of Counts's remarks made during the panel discussion. These remarks are a succinct summary of one of Counts's central themes—collectivism—already discussed; it is worthwhile to reproduce them:

Collectivism is here employed to characterize an economy marked by close integration, interdependence, and some form of unified control, coordination, and direction. Since the dissolution of the fairly self-contained rural household of the early years of the Republic, a relatively complete collectivism on a small scale, the trend toward a new integration which embraces the entire nation has advanced hand in hand with the movement of technology into the realms of transportation, communication, production, exchange, and government.

Already the new conditions seem throroly to have established themselves. The American people today experience a collectivism of prosperity, depression, and catastrophe. It is not a question of trend; it is a question of reality. It is a condition, not a theory, nor is it a hope.

... To my mind, the probability lies overwhelmingly in the direction of the continuation of the present collective pattern.... But this does not mean that the schools are forced to a narrow form of indoctrination as many critics have supposed. On the contrary, it provides a firm basis for an education with its feet on the ground of reality. Within the pattern of ever-closer integration, there are many possibilities. It is the function of the school to explore these possibilities— all of them—and help the younger generation to a solution that is in harmony with the ideals of American democracy. American educators may hesitate, but I am of the opinion that sooner or later they will find no other course open to them.[358]

These statements by Beard and Counts on the third day of the convention were, however, very small change compared with what Counts said earlier and what Beard said later. The newly formed John Dewey Society held its first annual meeting in St. Louis concurrently with the opening meeting of the Department of Superintendence. Counts was one of the main speakers that afternoon, and he created a stir. In his speech he returned to the by now familiar topic—a denunciation of Hearst, as well as of Frank Belgrano, former commander of the American Legion, Alfred E. Smith, Father Coughlin, and the Daughters of the American Revolution. To these he now attached the American Liberty League, whose purpose, he stated, "is so obviously that of protecting the great fortunes obtained through munitions sales, speculation and the expoitation of the American people."[359] This was too much for Jouett Shouse, president of the American Liberty League, and his protests carried Counts's name into the headlines of the *St. Louis Globe-Democrat* and his picture (tieless but wearing his best fighting face) into the top center of the front page. Shouse challenged Counts to cite authorities for his allegations. Counts issued a response immediately:

> You and your lawyers, representing great property interests, have attacked several great statutes enacted by the present government to cope with economic crisis and protect basic economic liberties of the people.
>
> Have you intervened in any one of many cases during the past 12 months involving freedom of speech, freedom of press, freedom of assemblage, freedom of religious worship, freedom of thought and teaching, right to fair trial of working men?

The reporter who was with Counts in his room at the Hotel Jefferson colorfully continued, "Counts jumped up out of his chair and paced back and forth in the hotel room with clenched fists deep in his pockets as he indignantly enumerated a few of the list of cases he was thinking of as he drafted his reply."[360]

Beard, probably in concert with Counts (remember that Counts was a Kansas boy), also took up the Hearst issue and sent off a wire to Governor Alfred Landon of Kansas, which began, "A number of American educators who have followed your career with deep interest would like to ask you one question: Are you proud to be sponsored by William Randolph Hearst?"[361] The basis for this challenge, Beard explained, dated back to the early years of the century when, following President McKinley's second election, the *New York Journal*, one of the Hearst papers, suggested that "[i]f bad men cannot be got rid of except by killing, then the killing must be done."[362] Beard considered this statement an invitation to assassination.

In his speech to the John Dewey Society, Counts had made reference to Beard's characterization of Hearst as "an enemy of everything that is noblest and best in our American tradition."[363] One of the least noble things that seemed to strike the educators meeting in St. Louis was the loyalty oath required of teachers. Counts himself was reported to say, "Children should be loyal, and taught loyalty, but saluting the flag and taking oaths of allegiance are an interference with educational processes by an outside force.

Teachers now are more nearly 100 per cent American than any other occupational group. If they cannot be trusted, then there is no hope for America."[364] The convention sent instructions to Frank Ballou in Washington to support the Sisson Bill, which was to repeal the notorious red-rider. The rider had been attached to a 1937 Appropriations Bill for D.C., and it required each teacher in the district, on receiving his or her pay, to make affidavit that he or she had not taught or advocated communism. The forces of re-actionism were not only very strong but were also effectively represented in high places.

Educational Policies Commission

Beard's and Counts's association with the NEA was not over, and within the next few years both brought out books under its auspices. At the annual meeting of the NEA in Denver in July 1935 an Educational Policies Commission was organized "to develop a constructive program for the continuous self-appraisal of the American system of education and to suggest means whereby changes for the improvement of our educational institutions might be more speedily accomplished."[365] Counts was appointed a member of the commission, and remained so until 1943. The members felt that their first task seemed to be to define the functions of education in a democratic society, and Beard was assigned the task of preparing a volume for the commission which appeared in 1937 with the title *The Unique Function of Education in American Democracy*. The first draft of the volume was distributed to members, which included Charles Judd. A second draft was discussed, amended, and approved after Beard had made revisions. The book, or report as it was called, "describes the influences thruout the history of America which were effective in shaping the public school system, and in that background reveals the unique contribution of education to the growth of a democracy. . . . [I]t makes clear that by virtue of this unique function, education must be accorded freedom from partisan politics and other special-interest controls in order that it may best discharge its obligations to society."[366] Counts called the book "a classic," and with some pride told Beard, "I am more than glad that I had something to do with getting you to undertake it."[367] A few months later Counts relayed to Beard the complimentary comments on the volume made by F.A. Spencer of New York University: "I shall not soon forget the enthusiasm with which I read 'The Unique Function of Education in American Democracy.' It is by all odds the noblest and finest document of its kind that I have ever seen. I was genuinely moved and inspired by it. I hope for it the widest possible currency and influence."[368]

Counts's volume, *The Education of Free Men in American Democracy*, was the major publication of the Educational Policies Commission for 1941.[369] It was approved unanimously by the commission members, which now did not include Judd. John W. Studebaker, still U.S. commissioner of education, gave the book a favorable review, and called it "stimulating and searching in its analysis of the contribution which education alone can make to the defense and achievement of human freedom."[370] The theme of the book is by now familiar. Studebaker described it as follows:

> The author is convinced that military and economic preparedness are probably the easiest part of the task of defending democracy in today's world. It is in the building of the spiritual ramparts of democracy that we face the more difficult task. Says he, "Democracy exists only in the patterns of behavior, feeling, and thought of the people. Let these patterns be destroyed and democracy is destroyed. And they will be destroyed if they are not acquired anew by each generation, required by the complicated process of teaching and learning." Hence the author's insistence that the American people "should fashion an education frankly and systematically designed to give the rising generation the loyalties, the knowledge, and the discipline of free men."[371]

In Counts's view, this was clearly indoctrination, and why not? Both the Beard and Counts books, together with a third by William G. Carr, were later reprinted together in one volume, in response to many requests.[372] The works of Beard and Counts were clearly associated in the minds of people.

Counts made a third trip—it was to be his last—to Russia in the latter part of 1936. On this occasion he was to see the darker side of communism—it was the time of Stalin's big purge—and Counts clearly backed away from the brink. His friend, the educator Albert Petrovich Pinkevich, was sent to a forced labor camp within a month after bidding Counts farewell at the railway station. The terror had become personalized. Later, Counts was to say that by the middle thirties "he came to the conclusion that in spite of its professions the Communist movement throughout the world is profoundly hostile to democracy, human liberty, and all the values of civilized life."[373] In place of *collectivism* Counts begins to use the phrase *democratic collectivism*, that had been used by Beard in 1933. He continued to sound the warning that began with his controversial chapter, "To Surpass America."[374] Soon after Counts's return, Beard welcomed him back and added, "Europe is a madhouse, and we need you at home."[375]

Proposal for Teachers College

Throughout the thirities Counts made several efforts to begin an institute of social research at Teachers College. As early as 1931, he had formulated his preliminary ideas in a letter to the dean, William F. Russell. Counts recognized that education rests on two foundations—psychology and social science. In the letter he writes, "Our schools are often ineffective because they recognize only the laws of individual learning and disregard the laws which govern social learning or social change. An institution devoted to the cause of education cannot continue to neglect to study the forces and factors which condition changes in culture and social structure."[376] In what appears to be an early draft proposal for such an institute, Counts writes, "A genuine teachers college should be a center of liberal culture—an institution devoted to the task of making education an instrument for the refinement and elevation of American life."[377]

In the spring of 1937, Counts again discussed the project with Dean Russell. The intention was "to promote a comprehensive and intensive inquiry over a period of years into the nature of the American democratic tradition and related matters. The object would be to secure guidance in the formulation of educational policy during the years ahead when American democracy is likely to pass through a period of crisis."[378]

Counts inevitably wanted to enlist Beard's active cooperation in the founding and running of the Teachers College institute, and he suggested to Russell that Beard might be interested. For his part, Beard noted that he was running from new obligations but readily agreed to meet with Counts and Russell. A meeting of the three men was arranged for the spring, which took place on May 25 at the Blue Bird Inn, ten miles from Bridgeport, Connecticut. Counts and Beard prepared draft proposals. Counts suggested an annual budget of $69,000 for the research program, which was to be organized around seven closely related but independent divisions:

1. The historical and cultural sources of American educational ideas.
2. The democratic process as it shapes and conditions American education.
3. American education as it shapes and conditions the democratic process.
4. The expectations of the American people regarding education.
5. The relation of education to social agencies and institutions.
6. The influence of the changing culture on human abilities and social idea.
7. The increasing demand of society upon the school.

Counts was enthusiastic: "Personally I believe it would make Teachers College a most significant institution of higher learning in America and would also change the conception of teacher-training and of education throughout the country. It looks like the most significant idea that has entered American education during our time."[379] On July 9, the two friends, together with Russell, Jesse Newlon, and Merle Curti, gathered at Beard's home in New Milford. "It was a grand jamboree we had at your place. Everybody on our side was delighted. Also we all came away feeling that real progress had been made and that the project is going forward. Of the latter there is no question."[380] Russell was still "tremendously interested."

During the last months of the year, work on the institute progressed, and Beard, in spite of some health problems, continued to make an important contribution but refused any payment for his efforts. By the following March, a major snag had developed. Beard alerted Counts to a *New York Times* article which announced plans by the University of Pennsylvania to offer "a new combination of graduate courses in American history and literature for students who wish to specialize in the broad field of the development of social and cultural institutions."[381] Nonetheless, the program, as described in the *Times,* seems to have been less on the lines of the proposed institute and more on the lines of a combination of literature and history. Gerald Gutek suggests that the efforts of Counts and the others to inaugurate the institute might have been reflected in the founding at Teachers College in 1938 of a separate Department of Social and Philosophical Foundations as Division 1 of the Foundations of Education.[382].

However, it should not be overlooked that the dean was not totally in favor of the Counts-Beard approach to educational reform. He had made his position quite clear in an address given at the meeting of the NEA's Department of Superintendence in New Orleans in February 1937. Russell explicitly mentioned Counts in an address he gave, and remarked that Counts played into the hands of the extremists on the right and left. People looking for Utopia will want an easily understood plan, which Counts and his associates did not have but which both the fascists and the communists do. "What we need is not attention [education] to the left or right, but education for the middle of the road."[383] In addition, Russell was not convinced that planning itself *could* bring about the change intended. "Who can tell whether a social change, most carefully planned, may not become, like the English sparrow in America or the European rabbit in Australia, nothing but a pest?"[384] Nonetheless, Lawrence Cremin and associates report on "the warm feeling of mutal respect and friendship which has always existed between Dean Russell and Professor Counts."[385]

Counts and the AFT

In September 1939, Counts was elected president of the American Federation of Teachers. He ran for the post against Beard's advice: "[S]tick to your own knitting and leave fist fights to those who are especially fitted for them."[386] It was by no means certain that Counts would win the election, since he had already been defeated in an attempt to win the presidency of New York Local 537, the college professors' local. However, on August 23, 1939, in the middle of the AFT convention, the Soviet-Nazi pact was signed, and Counts, somewhat modestly, suggested that, in light of the pact, many teachers voted for him who might not otherwise have done so. His first and perhaps his major task of the three years he held the position was to check the growing influence of a powerful communist minority within certain locals of the AFT. During his term the constitution of the federation was rewritten so as to eliminate from membership teachers who were also members of totalitarian parties, whether they were fascist or communist. Under Counts's leadership this was possible because no one could accuse him of right-wing sympathies.[387] Counts was proud to recall that he took the lead in one of the pioneering struggles to destroy the communist influence in American labor. The burden was heavy, and, in addition to continuing to fulfill his obligations at Teachers College, during his first year in office he gave about 110 speeches all over the country. He was pleased to witness the growing activism among teachers everywhere.

Another task that fell to Counts was to encourage union members to full participation in the war effort. Counts always held that the world, in the move of the developed countries from an agrarian to an industrial order, had returned to its original state: it was once again a Garden of Eden—not, of course, a Garden of Eden with respect to innocence, but in the sense that it was one interdependent entity. Events in Europe or Asia could not fail to affect the people of America, and vice versa.

Counts's other brush with communism occured during his tenure as chair of the American Labor Party from 1942-44. In this instance the left-wingers held sway, and Counts and others of his colleagues split off to form the New York Liberal Party, which its members hoped would become a national third party. Counts was an active member of the Liberal Party until he left New York, and he ran for the U.S. Senate under its auspices in 1952. He was defeated but did gain a half-million votes. He remained active in the affairs of the AFT, and was appointed a member of its Commission on Post-War Reconstruction. The result of this involvement was a small book, *America, Russia, and the Communist Party in the Postwar World*,[388] which he coauthored with John Childs. The book, although highly critical of communism, emphasized the importance of accommodation with Russia following the end of the war. The authors called on America to modify its historic policy of isolationism.

Beard's View of Roosevelt

In encouraging the war effort, Counts differed greatly from Beard, who strongly advocated America's nonparticipation in the war. This attitude earned Beard the disapproval of some of his former friends, such as his old collaborator, Lewis Mumford, who resigned from the International Institute of Arts and Letters in protest against Beard's receipt of the institute's gold medal, awarded only once every ten years. As Beale writes, "Some men who had loved Beard came to dislike him bitterly."[389] Counts, needless to say, was not among their number.

Beard's posture on noninvolvement did not spring so much from the reactionary isolationism so much deplored by Counts and Childs, but from a strong conviction that America's participation would damage the cause of democracy within the republic itself. He "abhorred Europe's interminable wars, long-cherished hatreds, and colonial adventures."[390] Yet, with all that, he had a great regard for the English people, and believed their country to be "the most civilized of nations."[391] Beard's criticisms of the president's policies grew during Roosevelt's White House years. He approved of the goals of Roosevelt's domestic policy in general, and not only worked for the National Recovery Administration,[392] but was also invited to become a member of the Commission of the Constitutional Sesquicentennial. This latter appointment Beard declined because it seemed to him that it was developing along political rather than historical lines. A letter of regret, personally signed by Franklin Roosevelt, was sent to Beard in the middle of January 1936. By this time, Beard, who had hitherto been on quite friendly terms with the president, began to be suspicious of his handling of foreign policy. He felt that Roosevelt's growing predilection for involvement in the affairs of other nations was partly a diversionary tactic on account of the growing failure of his domestic program, or the "New Shuffle," as Beard called the "New Deal." Beard's criticism of Roosevelt continued unabated during the war years, and culminated in the sentiments of his last book, completed only months before the president's death, *President Roosevelt and the Coming of the War, 1941.*[393] Counts, although remaining ever faithful to Beard, continued to be a staunch supporter of FDR.

Beard Returns to Columbia

At the same time that Counts assumed the presidency of the AFT, Beard returned for one semester to teach at Columbia—his alma mater. One of Beard's two seminars was on the concept of democracy in American political thought. It had been twenty-two years since he had resigned his teaching post there, amid considerable controversy. Since that time he had been more or less an exile from the academic world. His resignation, in 1917, was precipitated by the expulsion of three professors, Cattell, Dana, and Fraser, who opposed America's entry into the war, which Beard himself supported. The heart of the matter seems to have been Beard's growing conviction that the trustees were interfering in academic matters. As Beard put it in his letter of of resignation to President Butler on October 8, 1917, "Having observed closely the inner life at Columbia for many years, I have been driven to the conclusion that the university is really under the control of a small and active group of trustees who have no standing in the world of education, who are reactionary and visionless in politics and narrow and mediaeval in religion."[394] In later life, actually during the fall semester of 1939, when he once again joined the Columbia faculty, Beard maintained that the Fraser episode was the reason for his resignation. But, as a member of the small dinner party during which this position was maintained, John D. Millet records that Beard "said nothing about the accumulation of concerns that finally erupted in his decision to resign."[395] These concerns included some vociferous reaction, both within and without the university, on the publication in 1913 of the controversial and epoch-making *An Economic Interpretation of the Con-*

stitution of the United States.[396] Butler had been alerted to Beard, and a speech delivered by Beard to the National Conference on Community Centers held in New York on April 21, 1916 brought forth a reprimand from Columbia's president. On the day following the speech the *New York World-Telegram* published, in Beard's words, a "garbled report" of his speech, but the damage had been done. The front-page headline ran, "To Hell with the Flag, O.K., Says a Columbia Professor." As Beard tells it, one speaker at the National Conference of Community Centers had used the offending phrase about the flag. This had led other speakers to urge the closing of the school centers altogether. Beard took "the reasonable and moderate view that the intemperance of one man should not drive us into closing the school to others."[397] Butler suggested that Beard correct the wrong impression that had been created. This he tried to do by writing to the papers, but Beard was nonetheless summoned to appear before a committee of the trustees, before whom he had little difficulty, he thought, in clearing up the misunderstanding. However, Beard had hardly endeared himself to the trustees, and before he left the room an "inquisition" on his views and his teaching was launched. Beard was bitter that Butler took no steps to stop the questioning, although later Butler privately urged Beard to drop the matter. Beard was not about to do that, and he took the position that the faculty should be examined in matters of opinion only by their peers and not by the trustees. The issue of academic freedom was always one to which Beard reacted strongly. The search for truth, as he had pointed out in the *Charter*, had to go where it led and must never be suppressed by dogmas, doctrines, or vested interests.

All this had been buried, if not forgotten, by the time Beard received an honorary degree, Doctor of Letters, from Columbia in 1944. The formula read, "Historian and political scientist; trained at DePauw University; associated for many years with Columbia University where for a decade he was an honored professor of politics; guide and philosopher in many different undertakings and valued interpreter of the lessons of history." In his letter notifying Beard of the award, Nicholas Murray Butler, now quite blind and only a few weeks from retirement, wrote that the degree was being conferred "in recognition of your long years of distinguished academic service and your important contributions to the literature of our time."[398] Beard was obviously pleased to accept the honor and added, "In my haste to make this overdue acknowledgement, I must leave unsaid for the moment many things that arise in my heart."[399] Whether this was a graceful way to avoid reference to the old disagreements is not at all clear, but there is in this brief and formal exchange of letters none of the caustic quality that had characterized some of their earlier associations. In the academic year (1940-41) following the one spent at Columbia, Beard went as visiting professor of American history to Johns Hopkins University, where his old colleague Isaiah Bowman was now president. Again he encountered opposition to what was perceived as his antiwar posture, and members of the faculty publicly critized Beard's opposition to the Lend-Lease Bill. But Beard clearly undertook the assignment with his usual opitmism. He felt he would have "the chance I have long wanted to start the kind of program that we talked over with Russell. Maybe I can last long enough to get some bricks and straw on the ground and start a few students off."[400] In this letter to Counts, Beard added, "Here's hoping we may meet this side of the beautiful shore!"

Beard's semester assignment at Columbia, as a visiting professor of government, should have brought him into close contact with Counts and his family. But Counts was too much away on union business. During the early forties Counts was very much occupied with the work of the AFT, the concerns of all-out war, the chairmanship of the American Labor Party, and the duties that devolved on him as he assumed the chairmanship of the Division of Foundations of Education at Teachers College in 1942. Thus there was a hiatus in the close contact between Beard and Counts during this period. But early in 1944 the old friendship resumed its accustomed tenor. An obviously happy Beard writes to Counts, "It certainly is a delight to hear from you again after the lapse of years and all that has happened to turn the world upside down. . . . I shall want to have a big jaw with you on the shape of the universe and what's doing or cooking now."[401]

Contact Renewed

Now that contact had been made, Counts resumed his practice of sharing some of his work with Beard. In September 1944, he asked Beard to look over the manuscript of his Kappa Delta Pi lecture, entitled *Education and the Promise of America*. "I would prize your judgment far beyond that of any other person."[402] Counts acknowledged Beard's help in the book's preface, in which he told the readers that Beard "read the manuscript with care and gave me many invaluable suggestions."[403] In the same place, Counts referred to Beard and Dewey as "our two most profound students of American democracy and the two greatest teachers of my generation."[404]

Against the backdrop of the closing weeks of the war, Counts was not blinded to the problems of victory. He saw that Russia and America would be rivals for the affections of common people all over the world. America, if she were to win those affections, would need to stand firmly by her professions. Here education performs a critical role as it examines the fundamentals of the country—its diversity, its commitment to democracy, and its geography. Then Counts, yet again, looks at the realtities of the age, which derive in large part from the emergence of an industrial civilization, which had brought in its train new modes of living and association. Tensions will be inevitable as the old and the new collide; we must look to our commitments to the Herbraic-Christian tradition, to the humanistic spirit, to the scientific method, to democracy, to world peace. We must not shirk the obligation to provide an expanded and enlarged education, one that promotes individual maturity and excellence, a society of free and equal people, a cooperative society (now Counts avoids that offending word *collectivist*), an economy of plenty, an enduring civilization of beauty and grandeur, an emerging world economy, a democratic constitutional government. That combined obligation presents enormous challenges to the teacher: "It requires of him . . . a deep understanding of our developing civilization in both its historical and its world setting. It requires . . . that he be sensitive to the profound moral implications of his calling—that he strive to express in his own life and work, both as teacher and as citizen, a great conception of American civilization."[405] This small book contains no new message from Counts, although it is, as always, beautifully expressed.

Counts sent Beard a copy of his book as soon as it was released the following spring. Beard thought the published version a substantial improvement over the draft and "a splendid antidote to the dogmas of the Adler-Hutchins-Lippmann-Van Doren output."[406] A few weeks later, Beard referred Counts to the review in the *New York Times*. Francis Hackett described the book as "arresting and powerful" and "a notable addition to the Kappa Delta Pi lecture series," and drew attention to the fact, which surely would have pleased both Counts and Beard, that Counts "is constantly aware of American history, being steeped in it."[407]

The war was drawing to a close, and Counts once more took a look at Russia and her education. Prior to publication he sent his article "Remaking the Russian Mind"[408] to Beard. Beard thought highly of it and wrote, "The article is beautiful in its informative force; if there is a waste word in it, I have not found it. Mary and I have both read it with deep interest."[409] Beard also complimented Counts on his article, "Russians Still Get Marxist View of Us," which not only apeared in the *New York Times*[410] but was reprinted in the *Congressional Record*.[411] "It was just the thing; no name calling or backbiting, just plain facts—and facts very important for the American people."[412] Counts, through these and numerous other activities, had reestablished himself as *the* American expert on Russian education. He anticipated a trip to Russia in May of 1946, but it did not materialize. Counts retained a deep affection for the Russian people while increasingly decrying their government. He maintained his dream of a return to Russia even into old age.

Rather than a trip to Russia, 1946 occasioned a trip to Japan. Counts was invited to serve on the Education Commission to Japan, whose purpose was to advise General MacArthur on the reconstruction of Japanese education. In preparation for this assignment, Counts visited Beard in order to discuss with him Beard's own Japanese experiences. He found the discussions "extremely helpful."

The Beard family first visited Japan in 1922 as highly honored guests, and remained several months. They returned to the United States the following summer, having travelled by way of Formosa, China, Korea, and Manchuria. They had not been home many weeks before the first wave of the great Tokyo earthquake struck on September 1. Within hours Beard had been cabled, "Come at once—we need your help." By October 5, Charles and Mary Beard were back in Tokyo helping with the reconstruction of the wrecked city. Beard was highly regarded by the Japanese, and was invited back in 1948. He declined, probably on account of his failing health. Both Beard and Counts developed a great affection for Japan, for the country and its people. Possibly Beard's personal knowledge of Japan and some of her leading statesmen reinforced his opposition to Roosevelt's developing anti-Japanese policies.

Beard's Death

During the postwar years, Counts continued to visit Beard at his home in the hills of Connecticut, and also at his winter retreat at the Pine Crest Inn, in North Carolina. Shortly after the explosion of the first atomic bomb on Hiroshima on August 6, 1945, Counts spent an afternoon at New Milford. In response to a question posed by Counts concerning the survival of the human race, Beard responded, "The human race will survive all right, it has been a long and tough journey. It will survive." Counts continues, "'Well,' I said, 'I am a little surprised that you would say that.' 'Well, I am not saying that we will not have a catastrophe that will set us back 2,000 years, but the human race will survive.'" Counts could not help adding, "I think that is close to zero in the scale of optimism."[413]

In the summer of 1946, the Chinese ambassador to the United Nations, Dr. P.C. Chang, asked Counts if he could meet Beard. Beard was agreeable, of course, and Counts related the incident in later years:

I took my car and drove Dr. Chang up to New Milford. And Beard's house was on a great ridge overlooking the Potomac [Housatonic] River and there was a veranda in front of the house and we were sitting that afternoon the three of us on the veranda when Chang put this question to Beard. "Has America contributed anything to the advancement of civilization?" And Beard answered immediately and I think that question had been put to him by others; he had been over a good part of the world and I know that he had been asked to respond to that question many times. So he answered it immediately.

"Yes, I think we have contributed two things. First, we have contributed greatly to the development of technology that has lifted the burden of toil from men, women, youth and children. And secondly, we established a regime of liberty, political liberty, over a vast area and that constitutes our contribution."[414]

George Counts and his wife, Lois, were among the last, if not the last, of Beard's friends to visit Beard before his death on September 1, 1948. This is how Counts recalled that final, and for him very precious, memory of his "agreeable" companion:

This was in July 1948, about the 25th of July. Mrs. Counts and I drove up to New Milford to see him and his wife, Mary, and we spent the afternoon with them in his home and I was walking out to the car to drive back to New York, he came with me. And the last words he ever said to me were these. "Tell my former friends," and he emphasized the word 'former,' "that the old man looks like he might live ten years more." Well, he went to the hospital on the first of August and never came out. But he had been very severly criticized by some of his former friends for the position that he had taken on the Second World War.[415]

Beard's illness, eventually diagnosed as aplastic anemia, struck him during the latter part of July. On August 2 he was driven by ambulance to the Grace-New Haven hospital. "I'm in good shape," he protested as he was carried out on a stretcher, "but I have an eye infection. It feels like someone has driven a spike in my eyes and left it there."[416] The last thing he inquired about was his hearing aid.

Perhaps the most touching and certainly the most public tribute from Counts to Beard is found in Counts's chapter in Beale's book. Taken with the letters, it also reveals much of Counts himself as the private man. Very rarely did Counts permit his inner self to be put on view. It is in these two repositories.

As a sort of postscript, it is appropriate perhaps to note that Counts, on the publication of the Beale book on Beard, received from his old colleague August Krey a favorable appraisal of his chapter. Counts's response is characteristic: "It would be delightful to sit down over a stein of beer and discuss, not only the old days, but also the new days. With your broad historical perspective you might raise my spirits a bit. To me things look pretty dark for free institutions. Perhaps the threat of atomic war and totalitarian triumph will soon pass away."[417]

To the end of his life, Counts talked affectionately of Beard, and in one of his last writings, "A Humble Autobiography," he refers to the association. Perhaps, however, the most telling story about these two agreeable people is related by Counts in his chapter in the Beale book.[418] The incident goes back to the early days of their friendship, to the fall of 1931 when they were motoring over the hills of Connecticut near the Beard home in New Milford:

Having been profoundly impressed by the vast range of his knowledge and thought, a range that seemed to embrace the entire human record from ancient times, I asked how long it would take him to tell all he had learned from his lifetime study of history. After contemplating the question a few moments he replied that he "thought" he could do it in "about a week." We drove on a short distance in silence. Where-upon he said he could probably do it in a day. After another brief pause, he reduced the time to half an hour. Finally, bringing his hand down on his knee, he said: "I can tell you all I have learned in a lifetime of study in just three laws of history. And here they are:

"First, whom the gods would destory they first make mad.

"Second, the mills of the gods grind slowly, yet they grind exceed-ingly small.

"Third, the bee fertilized the flower that it robs."

About ten days later we took a stroll along Riverside Drive in New York City. Evidently he had been giving further thought to my question. At any rate, he said he would like to add a fourth law to his laws of history:

"When it gets dark enough you can see the stars."[419]

Conclusion

The foregoing records the collaboration of two people who were in the thick of the educational fray during the 1930s. It records also the genesis of the historical basis of Counts's social reconstructionism, which was founded squarely on Beard's historiography. Its philosophical basis was Dewey's experimentatlism. Counts himself was a colleague of Dewey, but he was not a philosopher, and, indeed, at the University of Chicago took only one course in philosophy, and that was long after Dewey had left Chicago for Columbia. To Counts's close colleague, John L. Childs, fell the task of elucidating and elaborating the philosophic foundations of social reconstructionism.

Dewey's work has not been much mentioned thus far, but it should be evident that his philosophy, particularly in its educational focus, forms a backdrop for the entire period. But the Progressive Education Association, at certain points false to Dewey as it might have been, did not survive Beard's death by many years. Thorndike's mathematical measures left Dewey's ideas well behind in the race for educational favor. The testing people on the AHA Commission may have received short shrift from Beard and Counts, but that was not even a temporary setback on their triumphant march through twentieth century American education. Even today, measurement is the dominant theme for reformers of all kinds. Purpose, beyond national primacy in world affairs, is barely discussed.

What is perhaps less obvious than Beard's influence on Counts is Counts's influence on Beard. Richard Hofstadter, the most perceptive commentator on Beard's work, states: "In the early and middle

1930's Beard underwent an intellectual conversion from a firm adherence to the economic interpretation of history to a form of historical relativism that proved impossible to square with his earlier views. It is hard to say whether this conversion owed anything in the beginning to misgivings about his own work; but it clearly arose in good part out of the disillusionments and fears that came with the 1929 crash and the Great Depression, events which impelled him to reconsider his ideas about the nature of historical writing."[420] Hofstadter suggests that this change may have come about by Beard's growing familiarity with the work of Heussi, Croce, and Mannheim. There is no need to dispute that suggestion. However, there seems little doubt in the face of the evidence presented earlier that Counts, with his own set of predilections and his social agenda, also influenced Beard. Hofstadter adds a telling comment as he summarizes Beard's position: "Each one is locked into a frame of reference. The truth of a historical work is not timeless or unviersal but relative to the setting in which it was written; and it can be understood only in that setting."[421] Hofstadter may not have read Counts, for he makes no reference to him in his discussion of Beard, but Counts similarly states that "education is always a function of some particular civilization at some particular time in history"[422] and that it cannot be understood any other way. Or one can quote from the *Conclusions and Recommendations*, which was coauthored by Beard and Counts: "[E]ducation always has a geographical and cultural location; it is therefore specific, local, and dynamic, not general, universal, and unchanging; it is a function of a particular society at a particular time and place in history; it is rooted in some actual culture and expresses the philosophy and recognized needs of that culture."[423]

Together the careers of Counts and Beard covered almost three quarters of the twentieth century; those careers were both glorious and influential. But their story also demonstrates some difficulties of educational reform. As has been seen, some of the best minds, situated in the most prestigious and well-placed positions, supported by powerful allies, some not even mentioned here, able to command the front pages of great daily newspapers and columns in the *Congressional Record*, skillful enough to address audiences in the thousands, masters of the spoken and written word, teachers of a long procession of students from home and abroad, and committed to the common good, could not influence educational practice in substantial ways. Educational reform is never easy. Is it even possible unless it is initiated by the state? That question may in fact have been answered by Counts in one of his articles that he sent to Beard:

> The furious course of education in the Soviet Union is a direct result of the conception of education held by the Soviet leaders. To them education is an extremely serious business. It is regarded as an instrument of the Communist Party—an instrument through which the Party achieves its purposes. In this respect the system of education enjoys the same status as the military police, the armed forces, the state Planning Commission, or even the Soviet Government itself. The Party gives the closest attention to education and initiates through its decrees, resolutions and directives all important changes in policy. The slightest opposition to or criticism of such changes on the part of teachers or educators would result in dismissal and disgrace. No teacher, as a teacher, would presume to participate in the shaping of the broad purposes of education. He regards himself as a technician under obligation to translate into programs the policies formulated by the Party. Consequently, education in the Soviet Union has followed closely the course of the political struggle. As the revolutionary forces have taken new directions, confronted new conditions and assumed new tasks, the method and purposes of education have changed. In considering the future the student of Soviet education should ever keep in mind that the revolution is not yet completed.[424]

One reason the reformers of the 1930s had so little effect in practice may have been the Second World War. But that is too easy. True, Beard did not long survive the war—but Counts continued to be a powerful voice in education until well into the 1960s. The witch-hunts of the 1950s might have scared off some of the radical reformers, although they certainly did not inhibit Counts. Another reason might lie in the particular platforms form which the reformers spoke. Beard had no regular institutional affiliation after his 1917 resignation from Columbia, but he was well heard. Counts was based at Columbia University, as were many of his ideological colleagues, including Childs, Newlon, Kilpatrick, Rugg, and Dewey himself. Although Boyd Bode and H. Gordon Hullfish were at the Ohio State University, the movement was fairly localized. This centralization does not take into account the huge number of students that passed through the classes of these people. They spread not only across this country but also around the world, but they seemed not to have been able to effect second-order change either.

Although Counts was extremely aware of the political nature of education—all educational questions, he asserted, are basically political questions—he was apparently not interested in mapping out detailed strategies of change. He, like Beard, certainly involved himself in political activity, but men and women in teachers colleges throughout the country could hardly be expected to emulate them. Dan Lortie has briliantly pointed out the conservative orientation of the teaching profession as a whole,[425] and there is no reason to suppose that his postwar data are fundamentally different from those that might have been turned up in the 1930s. Counts, like Lortie, also recognized the passivity of teachers. Indeed, in one of the most celebrated passages in all of Counts's work he referred to teachers thus:

> Nothing really stirs us, unless it be that the bath water is cold, the toast burnt, or the elevator not running; or that perchance we miss the first section of a revolving door. Possibly this is the fundamental reason why we are so fearful of molding the child. We are moved by no great faiths; we are touched by no great passions. We can view a world order rushing rapidly towards collapse with no more concern than the outcome of a horse race.[426]

This is not to say that many teachers did nothing in response to the calls of the reformers. But, as Cuban writes,

> [T]eachers lacked the resources to do it all by themselves and needed technical assistance.
>
> Most teachers who endorsed progressive and informal educational ideas lacked access to that kind of aid or already felt overloaded with existing classroom demands. In a sink-or-swim fashion, most teachers who ventured into progressive and informal practices had to learn these skills by themselves, from like-minded colleagues either in school or elsewhere, from books, summer courses, etc.[427]

What changes they made were first-order changes.

One could make the case that fundamental second-order changes can not be undertaken by the educational establishment itself. It would take the power of the state (or possibly business) to effect second-order change. State influence is not necessarily benevolent, as Counts had seen. He wrote of the Soviet Union:

> When the Bolsheviks seized power and established the dictatorship, they found themselves ruling a vast conglomerate of peoples who neither understood nor shared their purposes. Indeed, among the educated classes they encountered widespread and bitter hostility. They resolved both to win the young in general and to rear a generation of specialists loyal to the revolutionary cause. The schools were

an indispensable instrument for the achievement of this double purpose. The Soviet leaders therefore could not liquidate the schools or the teachers as they might liquidate a parasitic class. They had to capture them.[428]

Such massive change does not occur in a heterogeneous, free society, and maybe that is just as well, for although benevolent change (if indeed that advocated by Counts, Beard, and their allies was benevolent) is not easy, neither then is malevolent change. But there is another explanation.

The conception of teaching and learning as giving and receiving information has a history that is centuries long. It is so deeply embedded in the thinking of the vast majority of people that all alternative conceptions (problem solving, project directing, leading students to the threshold of their own minds, learning to learn, the responsibility of knowing, and so on) are so strange that we have simply not given them sufficient time to catch on. Dewey hinted at this when he wrote that "the fundamental authoritarianism of the old education persists in various modified forms."[429] Dewey might echo the comment of the colonial writer who asked "why improvements in *education* have not kept place with improvements of every other kind." He concluded that "changes in the practice of men are always slower than changes in opinion."[430] It is just possible that the extensive, intensive, and profound efforts to bring about genuine change during the 1930s have simply not had time to be carried into action.

But it could also be that real second-order changes occur when we change our ways of thinking and perceiving. And that is almost the same point that Watzlawick and associates come to—that as we *see* problems in a new light we develop new tools to address them.[431] Counts and Beard were collaborators for change. Whether their strategies were right or wrong, wise or foolish, useful or useless, they certainly saw problems in a new light and thus brought about profound changes in our thinking. That is what makes them so important.

Bibliographic Note

Checklists of Beard's writings can be found in Bernard C. Burning's *Political and Social Thought of Charles A. Beard* (Seattle: University of Washington Press, 1962), pp. 257-89, and Ellen Nore's *Charles A. Beard: An Intellectual Biography* (Carbondale, IL: Southern Illinois University Press, 1983), pp. 287-97.

A checklist of Counts's writings can be found in *George S. Counts: Educator for a New Age*, ed. by Lawrence J. Dennis and William Edward Eaton (Carbondale, IL: Southern Illinois University Press, 1980), pp. 137-52.

Notes

1. C.A. Bowers, *Progressive Educator and the Depression* (New York: Random House, 1969), 114.

2. Gerald L. Gutek, *George S. Counts and American Civilization* (Macon, GA: Mercer University Press, 1984), 34.

3. Ibid., 157.

4. Richard Hofstadter, *Progressive Historians* (New York: Alfred A. Knopf, 1968), 177.

5. Ibid., 178.

6. Ibid., 218.

7. Ibid., 314.

8. Ibid., 308.

9. [George S. Counts], *A Call to the Teachers of the Nation* (New York: John Day, 1933), 21.

10. Charles H. Judd to George S. Counts, 23 June 1930, Charles H. Judd papers, University of Chicago Archives.

11. Hofstadter, 227-28.

12. Charles A. Beard to George S. Counts, 13 July 1945, Special Collections, Morris Library, Southern Illinois University at Carbondale.

13. *Charles A. Beard: An Intellectual Biography* (Carbondale and Edwardsville, IL: Southern Illinois University Press, 1983).

14. Seattle: University of Washington Press, 1962.

15. Filmed interview of Howard White with George S. Counts, 11 April 1972, City Colleges of Chicago.

16. Barry D. Karl, *Charles E. Merriam and the Study of Politics* (Chicago: University of Chicago Press, 1974), 186 seq.

17. George S. Counts, "A Humble Autobiography," in *Leaders in American Education*, ed. Robert J. Havighurst, Seventieth Yearbook of the National Society for the Study of Education, vol. 70, pt. 2 (Chicago: N.S.S.E., 1971), 170.

18. Beard to Counts, 25 December 1933, Special Collections, Morris Library, SIU-C.

19. John L. Childs, *American Pragmatism and Education* (New York: Henry Holt, 1956), 213.

20. For an exhaustive examination of Counts's years at the University of Chicago and the intellectual influences exerted on him during this critical period, see Charles D. Jay, *The Doctoral Program of George S. Counts at the University of Chicago (1913-1916): An Intellectual History* (unpublished dissertation, Southern Illinois University at Carbondale, 1982).

21. Counts was assisted by his secretary, Nucia P. Lodge, in writing this book, which was published by McGraw-Hill in 1957. It received the "Library and Justice Award" of the American Library Association. There was a prize of $5,000 attached to the award.

22. Eric F. Goldman, "Charles A. Beard: An Impression," in *Charles A. Beard: An Appraisal*, ed. Howard K. Beale (Lexington, KY: University of Kentucky Press, 1954), 6.

23. *Current Biography* (New York: H.W. Wilson, 1941), 177.

24. Ed. Clifton J. Phillips, "Charles A. Beard's Recollections of Henry County, Indiana," *Indiana Magazine of History* 55 (March 1959): 17.

25. Ibid., 19.

26. Ibid., 21.

27. *New Milford Times*, 2 September 1948.

28. Published by Macmillan in 1913.

29. Interview with Counts, part 4 [typescript], n.d., pp. 2-3, Special Collections, Morris Library, SIU-C.

30. Charles A. Beard, "Written History as an Act of Faith," *American Historical Review* 39 (January 1934): 221.

31. Ibid., 219.

32. Samuel Eliot Morrison, "Faith of a Historian," *American Historical Review* 56 (January 1951): 264.

33. Ibid., 268.

34. Merle Curti, "Beard as Historical Critic," in Beale, 207 seq.

35. Beale, 231-53.

36. Joseph Shafer, Untitled [typescript], p. 4, August C. Krey papers, University of Minnesota Archives. See also Edgar Dawson, *Teaching the Social Studies* (New York: Macmillan, 1935), 395-97.

37. Ibid.

38. Ibid., 9.

39. Ibid., 11.

40. Counts delivered the Fourth Annual Lecture on January 9, 1929; it was published under the title *Secondary Education and Industrialism.*

41. Edgar Dawson, "The History Inquiry," *Historical Outlook* 15 (June 1924): 239-72; and *The History Inquiry* (Philadelphia: McKinley Pubs. Co., 1924), 36 pp.

42. American Historical Association, *Annual Report* 1924 (Washington, D.C.: U.S. Government Printing Office, 1929), 84.

43. Ibid., 97.

44. Edgar Dawson to A.C. Krey, 3 February 1925, Records of the American Historical Association, Manuscript Division, Library of Congress.

45. American Historical Association, *Annual Report* 1925 (Washington, D.C.: U.S. Government Printing Office, 1929), 91.

46. Krey to Charles E. Merriam, 26 February 1927, Charles E. Merriam papers, University of Chicago Archives.

47. Ibid.

48. Counts's name is mentioned in connection with the work of the commission for the first time in a report dated November 18, 1926 that Krey prepared for the AHA. As an example of the sort of work the commission might undertake, Krey referred to a study by C. [*sic*] S. Counts of fifteen cities undertaken during Spring 1924 that showed that an average of about 40 percent of the population of high school age were enrolled in the public high schools. Krey was referring to Counts's *Senior High School Curriculum,* (Chicago: University of Chicago Press, 1926).

49. Counts to Krey, 20 January 1927, Krey papers, University of Minnesota Archives. Jesse Steiner, in a somewhat similar vein to Counts, early called for the removal of *history* from the title of the commission on the grounds that it would indicate an emphasis that was not intended [Minutes of the Commission, 7-8 November 1929, 2].

50. American Historical Association, *Annual Report* 1926 (Washington, D.C.: U.S. Government Printing Office, 1930), p. 128; and John S. Bassett et al., "History and Other Social Studies in the Schools," *Historical Outlook* 18 (March 1927): 121.

51. Dawson to Krey, 17 December 1928, Krey papers, University of Minnesota Archives.

52. Including all of the original nine, save Bassett, who died on January 27, 1928.

53. Two members of the commission, Evarts B. Greene and William Lingelbach, resigned in 1929 and were replaced by Carlton J.H. Hayes, who had been involved in the selection of Krey as chairman five years earlier, and Avery O. Craven, professor of history at the University of Chicago.

54. Oddly, Counts's name is omitted from the list of members appointed at that meeting in the *Report of Progress* of 1929, although it is included in a list sent by Krey to F.P. Keppel, director of the Carnegie Corporation, dated 3 January 1929. The omission is evidently an oversight.

55. Even though the Carnegie Corporation underwrote the major work of the commission, the Commonwealth Fund earlier provided two small grants totalling $9,000 which enabled the commission to initiate its investigations.

56. Edmund E. Day was absent. He had been appointed, along with the others, at Indianapolis, but did not assume his duties until 1930. There had been a mix-up over Day's appointment. He did not respond to the invitation and thus it was assumed that he had accepted. Krey, erroneously, recalled a rejection by Day. However, by the spring of 1930 Day was a fully fledged member of the commission. Henry Johnson was not present on the first day or Isaiah Bowman on the second.

57. Report of Progress, December 1927 to April 1928 [typescript], 1.

58. Counts to Krey, 8 January 1929, Krey papers, University of Minnesota Archives.

59. Beard to Krey, 9 January 1929, Krey papers, University of Minnesota Archives.

60. It is ironic that Keppel's behavior had, in part, precipitated Beard's resignation from Columbia University. Keppel and President Butler had,

Beard believed, encouraged the pacifist behavior of Leon Fraser and then abandoned him when his views were under attack.

61. Harcourt, Brace, and Co., 1928.

62. Beard to Krey, 12 March 1929, Krey papers, University of Minnesota Archives.

63. That, indeed, was the substance of the book Bessie L. Pierce wrote for the commission. It was entitled *Citizens' Organizations and the Civic Training of Youth* and appeared in 1933 as volume 3.

64. Minutes of the Second Meeting of the Commission, Washington, D.C. 29-30 March 1929, 2-5. Also attached to Beard's letter, 12 March 1929.

65. Beard quotes the letter on page 27 of the book he wrote for the commission, *Nature of the Social Sciences in Relation to Objectives of Instruction* (New York: Charles Scribner's Sons, 1934). In summarizing Adams's view, Beard writes, "Henry Adams thought some genius would discover the 'laws' of all history as Darwin had presumably disclosed the 'laws of evolution'" (p. 57). This was a view which Beard, of course, vigorously opposed.

66. Minutes of the Second Meeting of the Commission, Washington, D.C., 29-30 March 1929, 5.

67. Minutes of the Third Meeting of the Commission, New York City, 7-8 November 1929, 3.

68. Jesse H. Newlon to Krey, 5 May 1929, Krey papers, University of Minnesota Archives.

69. Counts to C.H. Judd, 30 October 1929, Judd papers, University of Chicago Archives.

70. Ibid.

71. Lionel Kochan, *The Russian Revolution* (New York: G.P. Putnam's Sons, 1971), 124-25.

72. Longmans, Green, 1930.

73. George S. Counts, *The Soviet Challenge to America* (New York: John Day, 1931).

74. Counts, "A Humble Autobiography," 162.

75. American Historical Association, *Annual Report* 1930 (Washington, D.C.: U.S. Government Printing Office, 1931), 41.

76. Beard to W.G. Kimmel, 12 April 1930, Krey papers, University of Minnesota Archives.

77. Beard to Kimmel, 27 April 1930, Krey papers, University of Minnesota Archives.

78. Transcript of Meeting, 18 October 1930, 36 (309).

79. Franklin Bobbitt to Krey, 22 September 1930, Records of the AHA, Manuscript Division, Library of Congress.

80. Bobbitt to Krey, 18 November 1930, Records of the AHA, Manuscript Division, Library of Congress.

81. Bobbitt to Krey, 22 September 1930, Records of the AHA, Manuscript Division, Library of Congress.

82. Max Ferrand to Krey, 28 November 1930, Records of the AHA, Manuscript Division, Library of Congress.

83. Charles A. Beard, *A Charter for the Social Sciences in the Schools* (New York: Charles Scribner's Sons, 1932).

84. Counts, Horn, and Newlon to Beard, 19 April 1930, Special Collections, Morris Library, SIU-C.

85. Ibid.

86. Beard to Krey, 27 July 1930, Krey papers, University of Minnesota Archives.

87. Beard to Krey, 1 September 1930, Krey papers, University of Minnesota Archives.

88. Counts to Krey, 19 September 1930, Krey papers, University of Minnesota Archives.

89. Transcript of Meeting, 16 October 1930, 3.

90. Ibid.

91. Ibid., 8.

92. Ibid., 9.

93. Transcript of Meeting, 18 October 1930, 18 (239).

94. Ibid., 19 (242).

95. Ibid., 25 (257).

96. Counts to Beard, 23 October 1930, Special Collections, Morris Library, SIU-C.

97. Jesse F. Steiner to Krey, 23 October 1930, Records of the AHA, Manuscript Division, Library of Congress.

98. Transcript of Meeting, 18 October 1930, 25-27 (257, 259, 262).

99. Beard recounted his Japanese experience both before and immediately after the great Tokyo earthquake in "The Awakening of Japanese Cities," *American Review of Reviews* 69 (May 1924): 523-27.

100. Transcript of Meeting, 18 October 1930, 41 (320). Beard reiterated this conclusion in his *Nature of the Social Sciences*, 174-77.

101. Transcript of Meeting, 18 October 1930, 42 (322).

102. Ibid., 44 (326).

103. Transcript of Meeting, 17 October 1930, 72 (85).

104. Ibid., 73 (88).

105. Ibid., 72 (85).

106. Transcript of Meeting, 18 October 1930, 47 (333).

107. Transcript of Meeting, 17 October 1930, 112 (181).

108. Ibid., 93 (134).

109. Ibid., 98 (147).

110. Ibid., 122 (206).

111. Ibid., 127 (218).

112. Ibid.

113. Ibid., 115 (188).

114. Merriam to Newlon, 11 February 1931, Merriam papers, University of Chicago Archives.

115. Transcript of Meeting, 17 October 1930, 105 (163).

116. Minutes of the Meeting of the Commission, Briarcliff Manor, New York, 16-18 October 1930, 8.

117. Ibid.

118. Beard, *Nature of the Social Sciences*, x.

119. Beard and Krey to Guy Stanton Ford, 6 April 1931, Records of the AHA, Manuscript Division, Library of Congress.

120. Beard to Krey, 19 April [1931], Krey papers, University of Minnesota Archives.

121. Beard to Counts, 23 April [1931], Special Collections, Morris Library, SIU-C.

122. Counts to Beard, 22 April 1931, Special Collections, Morris Library, SIU-C.

123. Boyd H. Bode to Krey, 23 April 1931, Records of the AHA, Manuscript Division, Library of Congress.

124. American Historical Association, *Annual Report* 1931 (Washington, D.C.: U.S. Government Printing Office, 1932), 38.

125. Beard to Krey, [ca. May 1932], Krey papers, University of Minnesota Archives.

126. Beard, *Charter*, 3.

127. Ibid., 11.

128. Ibid., 21.

129. Ibid., 34.

130. Ibid., 37.

131. Ibid., 47.

132. Ibid., 51.

133. Ibid., 53.

134. Ibid., 87.

135. Ibid., 90-91.

136. Ibid., 107.

137. Ibid., 94.

138. *New York Times*, 15 May 1932, sec. 4, 9.

139. Hollis L. Caswell, "Charter for the Social Sciences," *School Executives Magazine* 51 (July 1932): 487.

140. George A. Coe, "Charter for the Social Sciences in the Schools," *Religious Education* 27 (September 1932): 641.

141. William McAndrew, "Why Schools Lack Educational Significance," *School and Society* 35 (4 June 1932): 774-75.

142. Charles H. Judd, "Programs of Social Studies for the Schools of the United States," *Elementary School Journal* 33 (September 1932): 22.

143. Houghton Mifflin, 1924.

144. American Historical Association, *Annual Report* 1935 (Washington, D.C.: U.S. Government Printing Office, 1936), 12.

145. Counts to Krey, 27 December 1930, Krey papers, University of Minnesota Archives.

146. Counts, "A Humble Autobiography," 173.

147. A copy of the outline accompanied identical letters to Krey and Merriam, both dated 27 December 1930.

148. Newlon to Merriam, 12 May 1931, Merriam papers, University of Chicago Archives.

149. List accompanying Newlon to Krey, 10 February 1931, Krey papers, University of Minnesota Archives.

150. Merriam to Newlon, 15 May 1931, Merriam papers, University of Chicago Archives.

151. Ibid.

152. Newlon to Merriam, 7 July 1931, Merriam papers, University of Chicago Archives.

153. The average salary for a professor at this time was about $3,000.

154. Krey to Patty W. Washington, 19 November 1932, Records of the AHA, Manuscript Division, Library of Congress.

155. Ernest Horn to Ford, 24 September 1931, Krey papers, University of Minnesota Archives.

156. Newlon to Merriam, 7 July 1931, Merriam papers, University of Chicago Archives.

157. Merriam to Edmund E. Day, 15 July 1931, Merriam papers, University of Chicago Archives.

158. Beard to Krey, 26 July [1931], Krey papers, University of Minnesota Archives.

159. Newlon to Krey, 27 July 1931, Krey papers, University of Minnesota Archives.

160. Counts to Merriam, 28 July 1931, Merriam papers, University of Chicago Archives.

161. Merriam to Counts, 31 July 1931, Merriam papers, University of Chicago Archives.

162. Ibid.

163. Counts to Merriam, 5 August 1931, Merriam papers, University of Chicago Archives.

164. Counts to Beard, 12 September 1931, Special Collections, Morris Library, SIU-C.

165. Newlon to Merriam, 12 May 1931, Merriam papers, University of Chicago Archives.

166. Krey to Beard, 10 March 1932, Krey papers, University of Minnesota Archives.

167. Philip A. Knowlton to Krey, 10 February 1932, Records of the AHA, Manuscript Division, Library of Congress.

168. Memorandum from Krey to the President and Council of the AHA, [January 1932], 3.

169. Beard to Krey, 15 March [1932], Krey papers, University of Minnesota Archives.

170. Merriam's contribution was titled *Civic Education in the United States.*

171. Minutes of the Meeting of the Executive Committee, Chicago, 6 December 1931, 3.

172. Ibid., 2.

173. Krey to Beard, 12 December 1931, Krey papers, University of Minnesota Archives.

174. Beard, *Nature of the Social Sciences*, ix.

175. Beard to Counts, 24 December 1931, Special Collections, Morris Library, SIU-C.

176. Counts to Beard, 7 January 1932, Special Collections, Morris Library, SIU-C.

177. Beard to Counts, 3 March 1932, Special Collections, Morris Library, SIU-C.

178. Beard to Counts, 14 February 1932, Special Collections, Morris Library, SIU-C.

179. Chapters on technology and government.

180. Counts to Merriam, 8 December 1932, Merriam papers, University of Chicago Archives.

181. Beard to Counts, 7 February [1933], Special Collections, Morris Library, SIU-C.

182. Beard to Krey, 20 February [1933], Krey papers, University of Minnesota Archives.

183. Krey to Beard, quoted directly by Beard in Beard to Krey, 5 July [1933], Krey papers, University of Minnesota Archives.

184. Ibid.

185. Beard to Krey, 28 March [1933], Krey papers, University of Minnesota Archives.

186. Beard to Krey, 11 July [1933], Krey papers, University of Minnesota Archives.

187. Beard to Krey, 27 January [1933], Krey papers, University of Minnesota Archives.

188. Beard to Krey, 11 November [1932], Krey papers, University of Minnesota Archives.

189. Beard to Krey, 9 December [1932], Krey papers, University of Minnesota Archives.

190. Beard to Counts, [6 August 1933], Special Collections, Morris Library, SIU-C.

191. Beard to Counts, [25 November 1933], Special Collections, Morris Library, SIU-C. Written by hand on Counts's letter to Beard, 23 November 1933.

192. Beard to Krey, 16 December [1932], Krey papers, University of Minnesota Archives.

193. Beard to Krey, 27 January [1933], Krey papers, University of Minnesota Archives.

194. Ibid.

195. Beard to "my colleagues on the Commission," 4 February [1933], Records of the AHA, Manuscript Division, Library of Congress.

196. Beard to Krey, 25 July [1933], Krey papers, University of Minnesota Archives.

197. Transcript of Meeting, Fourth Session, 28 October 1932, 4.

198. Beard to Krey, 19 March [1933], Krey papers, University of Minnesota Archives.

199. Krey to Beard, 19 May 1934, Krey papers, University of Minnesota Archives.

200. Merriam to Counts, 28 June 1933, Merriam papers, University of Chicago Archives.

201. Krey to George M. Stephenson, 30 September 1933, Krey papers, University of Minnesota Archives.

202. University of Minnesota Press, 1936.

203. Maxine B. Clapp to Lawrence J. Dennis, 14 November 1980.

204. Columbia University Press, 1943.

205. Beard to Krey, 2 June [1944], Krey papers, University of Minnesota Archives.

206. Truman L. Kelley and A.C. Krey, *Tests and Measurements in the Social Sciences* (New York: Charles Scribner's Sons, 1934).

207. Ford to Counts, 5 February 1934, Krey papers, University of Minnesota Archives.

208. Counts to Krey, 18 October 1933, Krey papers, University of Minnesota Archives.

209. Transcript of Meeting, 12 October 1933, [9:00 a.m.], 19.

210. Transcript of Meeting, 13 October 1933, 9:00 p.m. [a.m.], 5.

211. Ibid., 6.

212. Ibid., 18.

213. Ibid., 23.

214. Transcript of Meting, 12 October 1933, [9:00 a.m.], 6.

215. Ibid.

216. Ibid., 14.

217. Ibid., 8.

218. Ibid., 18.

219. Ibid., 9.

220. Ibid., 10.

221. Ibid., 22.

222. Ibid., 23-24.

223. Transcript of Meeting, 12 October 1933, 2:00 p.m., 20.

224. Transcript of Meeting, 13 October 1933, 9:00 p.m. [a.m.], 1.

225. Ibid., 19.

226. Beard to Ford, 18 October [1933], Krey papers, University of Minnesota Archives.

227. Minutes of the Meeting of the Commission, Princeton, 21-22 December 1933, 1.

228. Beard to Krey, 30 January [1934], Krey papers, University of Minnesota Archives.

229. Peter A. Soderbergh, "Charles A. Beard and the Commission on the Social Studies 1929-1933: A Reappraisal," *Social Education* 31 (October 1967): 467.

230. Recorded in ibid, 468.

231. Bessie L. Pierce to Krey, 18 December 1933, Records of the AHA, Manuscript Division, Library of Congress.

232. American Historical Association, *Annual Report* 1935 (Washington, D.C.: U.S. Government Printing Office, 1936), 19.

233. Beard to Krey, 17 January [1934], Krey papers, University of Minnesota Archives.

234. Merriam to Krey, 9 March 1934, Merriam papers, University of Chicago Archives.

235. Krey to Keppel, 29 May 1934, Krey papers, University of Minnesota Archives.

236. Ibid.

237. Merriam to Krey, 9 March 1934, Merriam papers, University of Chicago Archives.

238. Krey to Keppel, 29 May 1934, Merriam papers, University of Minnesota Archives.

239. Counts to Merriam, 3 April 1934, Merriam papers, University of Chicago Archives.

240. Horn to Krey, 21 March 1934, Krey papers, University of Minnesota Archives.

241. Ernest Horn, "Another Chapter on Tests for the Volume of 'Conclusions and Recommendations,'" *Social Studies* 26 (January 1935): 13-22.

242. Horn to Krey, 22 March 1934, Krey papers, Univesity of Minnesota Archives.

243. Krey to Counts, 24 January 1934, Krey papers, University of Minnesota Archives.

244. Krey to Keppel, 29 May 1934, Krey papers, University of Minnesota Archives.

245. Merriam to Day, 9 December 1933, Merriam papers, University of Chicago Archives.

246. Frank W. Ballou to Newlon, 6 April 1934, Krey papers, University of Minnesota Archives.

247. *Congressional Record,* 80, Part 5 (2 April 1936):4837.

248. Ibid., 4839.

249. Ibid., 4858.

250. Beard to Counts, 25 March [1936], Special Collections, Morris Library, SIU-C.

251. *Philadelphia Record,* 6 July 1936. Reprinted in *Teachers College Student News,* 5 August 1936, 2.

252. Beard to Counts, 5 August 1934, Special Collections, Morris Library, SIU-C.

253. Beard to Counts, [ca. 10 August 1934], Special Collections, Morris Library, SIU-C.

254. Beard to Counts, 17 January [1934], Special Collections, Morris Library, SIU-C.

255. Harry Elmer Barnes, "The Liberal Viewpoint," *New York World-Telegram,* 1 February 1934, 20.

256. Harry Elmer Barnes, "Review of Books," *American Historical Review* 40 (October 1934): 97.

257. Barnes, "The Liberal Viewpoint."

258. [Charles A. Beard and George S. Counts], *Conclusions and Recommendations of the Commission* (New York: Charles Schribner's Sons, 1934), 5.

259. Ibid., 7.

260. Ibid., 9.

261. Ibid., 46.

262. Ibid., 63-64.

263. Ibid., 83.

264. Ibid., 114.

265. Quoted in Press Release by Frank W. Ballou, 21 May 1934, Krey papers, University of Minnesota Archives, 3 [typescript]. Also *School and Society* 39 (2 June 1934): 702.

266. John L. Childs, "Education as Statecraft," *Social Frontier* 1 (November 1934): 26.

267. "Comments on the Conclusions and Recommendations of the Commission on the Social Sciences" [typescript], Krey papers, University of Minnesota Archives.

268. Franklin Bobbitt, "Questionable Recommendations of the Commission on the Social Studies," *School and Society* 40 (18 August 1934): 201-8.

269. Krey to Beard, 1 October 1934, Krey papers, University of Minnesota Archives.

270. M.E. Haggerty, "The Low Visibility of Educational Issues," *School and Society* 41 (2 March 1935): 283.

271. Percival W. Hutson, Review, *Elementary School Journal* 35 (March 1935): 551.

272. Harold Lord Varney, "Class-War on the Campus," *American Mercury* 40 (April 1937): 462-72.

273. Beard to Counts, 4 May [1937], Special Collections, Morris Library, SIU-C.

274. Transcript of Meeting, 27 October 1932, First Session, 3.

275. Transcript of Meeting, 28 October 1932, Fourth Session, 5.

276. Ibid.

277. Counts to Beard, 29 September 1933, Special Collections, Morris Library, SIU-C.

278. Krey to Counts, 3 October 1933, Krey papers, University of Minnesota Archives.

279. Ibid.

280. M.D. Howe to Krey, 12 March 1934, Krey papers, University of Minnesota Archives.

281. Krey to Counts, 7 March 1934, Krey papers, University of Minnesota Archives.

282. Ibid.

283. George S. Counts, *Social Foundations of Education* (New York: Charles Scribner's Sons, 1934), vii.

284. Ibid., 548.

285. Ibid., 4.

286. Ibid., 507-8.

287. Ibid., 548-49.

288. Ibid., 556.

289. Ibid., 558.

290. *Social Studies* 27 (February 1936): 141.

291. *School and Society* 41 (2 March 1935): 303.

292. Harold U. Faulkner, Review, *American Historical Review,* 40 (July 1935): 754.

293. Krey to Beard, 29 January 1934, Krey papers, University of Minnesota Archives.

294. Beard to Krey, 30 January [1934], Krey papers, University of Minnesota Archives.

295. Beard, *Nature of the Social Sciences,* 20.

296. Ibid., 35.

297. Ibid., 173.

298. Ibid., 49.

299. Ibid., 123.

300. Adolf A. Berle, Jr., and Gardiner C. Means, *Modern Corporation and Private Property* (New York: Macmillan, 1932).

301. Beard, *Nature of the Social Sciences,* 155.

302. Ibid., 156.

303. Ibid., 179.

304. A.G.K., Review, *Saturday Review of Literature* 10 (24 March 1934): 583.

305. Barnes, *American Historical Review* 40 (October 1934): 97.

306. Edgar B. Wesley, Review, *Social Studies* 26 (February, 1935): 126.

307. American Historical Association, *Annual Report* 1935 (Washington, D.C.: U.S. Government Printing Office, 1936), 92.

308. *The History of the American People for Grammar Grades and Junior High School* (New York: Macmillan, 1918).

309. Transcript of Meeting, 17 October 1930, 127 (218).

310. Beard to Krey, 13 May [1934], Krey papers, University of Minnesota Archives.

311. Beard to Counts, 4 October [1934], Special Collections, Morris Library, SIU-C.

312. Counts to Beard, 12 September 1935, Special Collections, Morris Library, SIU-C.

313. Counts to Beard, 16 February 1934, Special Collections, Morris Library, SIU-C.

314. Beard to Counts, 23 February [1934], Special Collections, Morris Library, SIU-C.

315. Counts to Beard, 7 March 1934, Special Collections, Morris Library, SIU-C.

316. William H. Kilpatrick, "Launching The Social Frontier," *Social Frontier* 1 (October 1934): 2.

317. [Probably by Counts himself], "Biography of George Sylvester Counts" [typescript], n.d., 3, Special Collections, Morris Library, SIU-C.

318. *New York Times*, 17 September 1934, 19.

319. *Frontiers of Democracy* 10 (15 October 1943): 2.

320. *New York World-Telegram*, 26 October 1934. Quoted in *Social Frontier*, 1 (November 1934): 22.

321. *Philadelphia Teacher*, Philadelphia, PA, November 1934. Quoted in *Social Frontier* 1 (December 1934): 35.

322. *Condorcet and the Rise of Liberalism* (New York: Harcourt, Brace, 1934) by J. Salwyn Schapiro was reviewed by Mordecai Grossman in the January 1935 issue of the *Social Frontier*, 36-37. *Handbook of NRA*, 2nd. ed. (New York and Washington, D.C.: Federal Codes Inc., 1934), was not reviewed in the *Social Frontier*.

323. Beard to Counts, 15 October [1934], Special Collections, Morris Library, SIU-C.

324. *Social Frontier* 1 (December 1934): 28.

325. Bowers, *Progressive Educator and the Depression*, 97.

326. *DePauw Journal*, 25 February 1935.

327. Charles A. Beard, "Property and Democracy," *Social Frontier* 1 (October 1934): 14.

328. Ibid., 15.

329. George S. Counts, *Dare the School Build a New Social Order?* (Carbondale, IL: Southern Illinois University Press, 1978), 36.

330. *Social Frontier* 3 (June 1937): 269-71.

331. "The Court Issue: a Reply," *Social Frontier* 4 (October 1937): 10-12.

332. *Social Frontier* 4 (November 1937): 67.

333. "Emerson as an American Dream-er," *Social Frontier* 4 (December 1937): 75-79.

334. *The Social Studies Curriculum,* 14th Yearbook (Washington, D.C.: Department of Superintendence, National Education Association, 1936), 5.

335. "The Discussion of the Yearbook," *Social Frontier* 1 (April 1935): 5.

336. Ibid., 6.

337. Charles A. Beard, "The Quest for National Security," in *Proceedings* of the Seventy-Third Annual Meeting (Washington, D.C.: National Education Association, 1935), 514.

338. Ibid., 513.

339. "A Society for the Study of Education in Its Social Relations," *Social Frontier* 1 (April 1935): 3.

340. William H. Kilpatrick (ed.), *The Teacher and Society* (New York: D. Appleton-Century Co., 1937).

341. For a full summary of the founding of the society, see "Reflective Thought and Practical Action: The Origins of the John Dewey Society" by Henry C. Johnson, Jr., *Educational Theory* 27 (Winter 1977): 65-75.

342. *Time,* 11 March 1935, 28.

343. Jesse H. Newlon, "Freedom of Teaching," in *The Teacher and Society,* ed. Kilpatrick, 281.

344. *New York Times,* 25 February 1935, 18.

345. *New York American,* 26 February 1935, 1-2.

346. "The Superintendents Resolve," *Social Frontier* 1 (April 1935): 7.

347. Ibid.

348. "The City Room and the School Room," in *Proceedings* of the Seventy-Third Annual Meeting (Washington, D.C.: National Education Association, 1935), 604-5.

349. Ibid., 608.

350. W.A. Swanberg, *Citizen Hearst* (New York: Charles Scribner's Sons, 1961), 469.

351. *New York Times*, 24 December 1934, 2.

352. Ibid.

353. Ibid.

354. *New York Times*, 4 April 1935, 3.

355. *New York Herald Tribune*, 4 April 1935, 21.

356. "W.R. Hearst and the Press," *Social Frontier* 1 (February 1935): 3.

357. Charles A. Beard, "The Scholar in an Age of Conflicts," in *Proceedings* of the Seventy-Fourth Annual Meeting (Washington, D.C.: National Education Association, 1936), 443.

358. "Jury-Panel Discussion of 1936 Yearbook," in ibid., 455-56.

359. *St. Louis Globe-Democrat*, 24 February 1936, 5A.

360. *St. Louis Globe-Democrat*, 25 February 1936, 1A.

361. *St. Louis Globe-Democrat*, 26 February 1936, 9A.

362. Ibid.

363. *St. Louis Post-Dispatch*, 24 February 1936, 1C.

364. *St. Louis Post-Dispatch*, 26 February 1936, 4C.

365. *Youth Education Today*, 16th Yearbook (Washington, D.C.: American Association of School Administrators, 1938), 390.

366. Ibid., 392.

367. Counts to Beard, 8 March 1937, Special Collections, Morris Library, SIU-C.

368. Counts to Beard, 6 January 1938, Special Collections, Morris Library, SIU-C.

369. At the beginning of the book Counts points out that "[t]he term 'man' or 'men' is employed . . . in its general sense to include both sexes" (p. 1).

370. John W. Studebaker, "The Education of Free Men in American Democracy," *School Life* 27 (October 1941): 5.

371. Ibid.

372. *Policies for Education in American Democracy* (Washington, D.C.: Educational Policies Commission, 1946).

373. "Biography of George Sylvester Counts," 3.

374. Counts, *Soviet Challenge to America,* 3-17.

375. Beard to Counts, 6 March [1937], Special Collections, Morris Library, SIU-C.

376. Counts to William F. Russell, 19 January 1931, Special Collections, Morris Library, SIU-C.

377. "Some Thoughts on the Organization of an Institute of Social Research at Teachers College" [typescript and longhand], n.d., 13, Special Collections, Morris Library, SIU-C.

378. Counts to Beard, 28 April 1937, Special Collections, Morris Library, SIU-C.

379. Counts to Beard, 15 June 1937, Special Collections, Morris Library, SIU-C.

380. Counts to Beard, 14 July 1937, Special Collections, Morris Library, SIU-C.

381. *New York Times,* 13 March 1938, sec. 2, 4N.

382. Gerald L. Gutek, *Educational Theory of George S. Counts* (Columbus, Ohio: Ohio State University Press, 1970), 169-70.

383. "Educators Warned on Utopia Building," *New York Times,* 24 February 1937, 26.

384. Ibid.

385. Lawrence A. Cremin, David A. Shannon, and Mary Evelyn Townsend, *History of Teachers College Columbia University* (New York: Columbia University Press, 1954), 253 (footnote).

386. Beard to Counts, [ca. August 1939], Special Collections, Morris Library, SIU-C.

387. See William Edward Eaton, *American Federation of Teachers, 1916-1961* (Carbondale, IL: Southern Illinois University Press, 1975), chapter 5.

388. John L. Childs and George S. Counts, *America, Russia, and the Communist Party in the Postwar World* (New York: John Day, 1943).

389. Beale, vi.

390. George S. Counts, "Charles Beard, the Public Man," in Beale, 235.

391. Ibid.

392. The announcement was made on September 16, 1933 that Beard had become a member of the Consumers Advisory Board. *New York Times,* 17 September 1933, 30.

393. Yale University Press, 1948.

394. Reported in the *New York Times,* 9 October 1917, 1.

395. John D. Millet, "Recollections of Charles A. Beard" [typescript], 6, Archives and Special Collections, DePauw University.

396. Macmillan, 1913.

397. Charles A. Beard, "A Statement by Charles A. Beard," *New Republic* 13 (29 December 1917): 249.

398. Nicholas Murray Butler to Beard, 7 March 1944, Archives and Special Collections, DePauw University.

399. Beard to Butler, 16 March 1944, Archives and Special Collections, DePauw University.

400. Beard to Counts, 8 November [1940], Special Collections, Morris Library, SIU-C.

401. Beard to Counts, 28 January [1944], Special Collections, Morris Library, SIU-C.

402. Counts to Beard, 28 September 1944, Special Collections, Morris Library, SIU-C.

403. George S. Counts, *Education and the Promise of America* (New York: Macmillan, 1945), vii.

404. Ibid.

405. Ibid., 156.

406. Beard to Counts, 27 March [1945], Special Collections, Morris Library, SIU-C.

407. "Books of the Times," *New York Times,* 10 May 1945, 21.

408. It was not, as Counts stated in Beale's volume, "Recent Changes in Soviet Education," which appeared in the *Educational Forum* 10 (May 1946), 423-36.

409. Beard to Counts, 13 July 1945, Special Collections, Morris Library, SIU-C.

410. *New York Times,* 7 October 1945, 24.

411. 91, Part 12 (9 October 1945): A4210-11.

412. Beard to Counts, 15 October 1945, Special Collections, Morris Library, SIU-C.

413. Interview with Counts, part 3 [typescript], n.d., 4, Special Collec-

tions, Morris Library, SIU-C. The spelling and punctuation errors in this unedited transcript have been corrected.

414. Ibid., part 4, 7-8.

415. Ibid., 3.

416. *New Milford Times,* 2 September 1948.

417. Counts to Krey, 23 July 1954, Krey papers, University of Minnesota Archives.

418. There is no reason to doubt the story as recounted by Counts, in spite of the existence of several variations. A letter from Carl Sandburg to Beard likened the four laws to poetry [Carl Sandburg to Beard, 22 February 1940, Archives and Special Collections, DePauw University]. Norman Cousins states that they were first relayed to a student. Shortly after Beard's death the "four laws" were reprinted in the *Waycross (Georgia) Journal-Herald,* 17 September 1948, where they contain an amusing lapsus that Beard would surely have relished: "The bee fertilizes the follower [*sic*] it robs."

419. Counts, in Beale, 251-52.

420. Hofstadter, 304.

421. Ibid., 307.

422. Counts, *Education and the Promise of America,* 23.

423. [Beard and Counts], *Conclusions and Recommendations,* 31.

424. Counts, "Remaking the Russian Mind," *Asia and the Americas* 45 (October 1945): 478.

425. Dan C. Lortie, *School-Teacher* (Chicago: University of Chicago Press, 1975).

426. Counts, *Dare the School,* 19-20.

427. Larry Cuban, *How Teachers Taught* (New York: Longman, 1984), 255.

428. Counts, "Remaking the Russian Mind," 479.

429. In Cuban, 257.

430. *Weekly Magazine* (Philadelphia, 4 August 1798): 12-13.

431. Paul Watzlawick, John H. Weakland, and Richard Fisch, *Change* (New York: W.W. Norton, 1974).

Index

191